HEALING FROM
A NARCISSISTIC RELATIONSHIP

HEALING FROM
A NARCISSISTIC RELATIONSHIP

A Caretaker's Guide to Recovery, Empowerment, and Transformation

Margalis Fjelstad

ROWMAN & LITTLEFIELD
Lanham • Boulder • New York • London

Published by Rowman & Littlefield
A wholly owned subsidiary of The Rowman & Littlefield Publishing Group,
Inc.
4501 Forbes Boulevard, Suite 200, Lanham, Maryland 20706
www.rowman.com

Unit A, Whitacre Mews, 26-34 Stannary Street, London SE11 4AB

British Library Cataloguing in Publication Information Available

Library of Congress Cataloging-in-Publication Data Available

ISBN: 978-1-4422-7200-2 (cloth : alk. paper)
ISBN: 978-1-4422-7201-9 (electronic)

∞ ™ The paper used in this publication meets the minimum requirements of
American National Standard for Information Sciences—Permanence of Paper
for Printed Library Materials, ANSI/NISO Z39.48-1992.

Printed in the United States of America

"We must be willing to let go of the life we planned
so as to have the life that is waiting for us."
E. M. Forester

AUTHOR'S NOTE

The examples, anecdotes, and characters in this book are drawn from my clinical work, research, and life experiences with real people and events. Names and some identifying events and details have been changed, and some situations are composites to protect people's privacy.

Throughout the book I consistently use masculine pronouns when talking about the narcissist. This is for ease of writing, instead of *he or she*, and because it is estimated that approximately 70 percent of narcissists are male. If the narcissist in your life is female, all of the comments and suggestions here will also apply.

CONTENTS

INTRODUCTION

Relationships with narcissists can be painful, frustrating, complicated, and totally mystifying. Nothing they say or do seems to be the same from day to day. They can be charming and loving one moment and hateful and demeaning the next. They tell you one thing and then do another. When you confront them with these discrepancies, they blame you and say you're the crazy one, and often you do end up feeling like you're crazy. The narcissist can swing you from emotional highs to emotional lows. Most relationships with narcissists can be described as follows in the next few paragraphs.

The relationship started out almost as a fairy tale. In the beginning you felt adored, understood, ecstatic, and more smitten than you had ever felt before. You thought that the two of you were completely in tune and that you even shared the same thoughts, feelings, and dreams. Your partner described to you the perfect life you would share together, more wonderful than you would have dared to dream of on your own. You felt a oneness. The relationship progressed very quickly, and within days, you were deeply and irrevocably in love. The narcissist told you this was the perfect relationship, and you committed yourself entirely.

But something changed after that—it may have been almost instantly or may have taken a few months or longer. Your oneness didn't seem to be there anymore. Your loved one became controlling, selfish, angry, blaming, and self-justifying. You no longer felt understood, and your needs seemed to be discounted and even mocked. You began to feel unheard, unappreciated, frustrated, and often depressed and anxious. You had to work hard to ignore your feelings of hurt and rejection.

You tried to talk about your feelings and needs, only to be treated as if your requests were silly, unimportant, or just plain foolish. You ended up wondering what was wrong with you. What had you done to make your loved one so distant and indifferent? You kept trying. You made accommodations. You gave more love and attention. You gave in to keep the peace. You gave up your interests and even time with your friends and family to meet your loved one's expectations. You tried in every way to be the perfect spouse or partner. And you kept hoping to get that loving feeling to return.

It was so confusing. You started to feel as though your whole life was being controlled by this person. Why was your partner being so mean and self-centered? You wanted your needs to be considered. You wanted to feel cared about. You wanted the relationship to be more equal and shared. You tried to do everything perfectly, and when that didn't work, you tried harder. Nothing seemed to make a difference for very long. You continually felt like the giver, your partner always demanding and taking more. And you often felt guilty that you weren't doing enough and couldn't get it right.

The longer you're in a relationship with someone so self-centered and self-absorbed, the more you feel drained, disappointed, and hurt. His selfishness pushes you away, but something inside of you keeps hoping things will change and he'll again be the person you know he can be—the funny, smart, caring person you first met but who now seems to be buried most of the time.

Along the way you saw hopeful signs. Your partner would suddenly be just as sweet and loving and attentive as you remembered. You felt that surge of happiness and relief that things were going to be all right after all. But all too quickly he switched back into anger and blame, ignoring and criticizing you when everything didn't go perfectly. Through all of this you kept hoping things would work out, and you kept working hard to be loving and kind to prove how much you wanted to make the relationship succeed.

Then one day your loved one announces that the relationship just is not working. It's no longer fulfilling or exciting. You're too negative and needy. You're boring and uninteresting. What? You are shocked and wonder if he's kidding you. You tried all this time to be as perfect, loving, accommodating, and giving as humanly possible, and that wasn't enough? You discounted your own needs and wants to make the relationship work, and even that wasn't sufficient. You denied your own feelings of dissatisfaction and kept trying to be positive and optimistic. Now, he says it's your fault. You didn't give enough, or you complained too much, or you weren't interesting enough, or sexy enough, or whatever enough. You've just been dumped by a narcissist.

Over my thirty-plus years of working as a marriage and family therapist, I have witnessed many such scenarios. And I, too, was once dumped by a narcissist. The experience is mind-numbing and devastating. Over the years it has been my purpose to comfort and heal the family members who are negatively affected by a loved one with narcissistic personality disorder.

So many people, including therapists, try to figure out *why* narcissists do what they do, and there are hundreds of books on that subject. I wrote my first book, *Stop Caretaking the Borderline or Narcissist*, because there was little written for people who found themselves enmeshed in a relationship with a narcissist or borderline person. I wanted family members to know that they were being seen and heard. I wanted to tell them there are defined patterns of thinking and feeling that create these insane dramas that they get drawn into. I wanted to show them they could get out of the drama. I also wanted them to know they could not fix or cure their narcissistic family member but that they could stop buying into the narcissist's insanity and learn to make a better life for themselves.

This book goes a step further. It's about healing and becoming whole and healthy again after a narcissistic relationship. I did it, and I have helped thousands of people find understanding, learn new skills, and heal in my Caretaker Recovery groups. When you're in a close relationship with a narcissist, you inevitably give up yourself, your dreams and opinions, and even your sense of individuality. You fall into what I call a "caretaker pattern," one in which you give up your needs to take care of what the narcissist needs and wants. You have to reverse this pattern in order to regain your emotional health. This book shows you how to do just that.

Recovering from a narcissistic relationship can take a lot longer than getting over the end of a typical relationship, because you've been on high alert, hypervigilant, and attuned to his every expectation or reaction. It will take some time for your stress hormones to become normal again. You may find that you feel exhausted and have to regain your strength. Most of all, you'll need to rebuild your sense of self and self-worth. No one gets out of a relationship with a narcissist unscathed.

If you feel confused and mystified, then this book will help you see things more clearly. If your self-esteem is in shambles, it will show you how to heal your wounds and regain your strength. If you wonder why all this happened, you'll find information and understanding. If your self-confidence has evaporated, you'll find encouragement. If you don't know where you're going from here, this book will give you direction.

If you have been through this same kind of relationship before, now is the time to break the pattern of taking care of others while ignoring and giving up yourself. Out of this experience you can learn better self-care and self-love. You can heal and recover your strength. You can break out of the self-sacrificing caretaker pattern forever and become more resilient than you ever were before. You may even find a new purpose and energy and maybe even a new you. It is never too late to choose again, begin again, and make a better life for yourself.

I

The Narcissist and the Caretaker

I

IT'S ALL ABOUT *THEM*—NARCISSISTS

"Here's the need to know revelation about narcissists: Whatever they do, it's never about you."
—Kathleen Parker, newswoman, the *Washington Post*

IN THE BEGINNING

When you first met and fell in love with the narcissist in your life, you were attracted to the charming, confident, easygoing, superfriendly way he appeared to be in the world. You probably felt really valued and enveloped in the center of his attention—rather like you were the only two people in the world. You felt special, selected, exceptional, or even privileged to have the attention of someone so fully and completely. You may actually have fallen in love in those first few moments.

WHAT A NARCISSIST SHOWS YOU

Usually within the first session with a client, I will be asked "Is my husband/wife really a narcissist?" The second question is, "Will he/she ever get better?" To answer the first question, let's look first at the behaviors and traits that identify narcissism. In chapter 3, I'll cover information on why narcissists rarely get better.

Narcissists create a glamorized "False Self," or persona, to show to the world.[1] This image of superiority and friendliness is usually easygoing and sociable. When a narcissist sets his sights on you and turns on the charm, it is almost mesmerizing. The attention and solicitude feel so good. You may get pulled in by his superior disdain for the conventional and mundane, which can appear contemporary and edgy. You feel cool and exclusive to be included in his world. When Amy met Chuck, she was impressed by his knowledge and confidence about seemingly everything. This gave her a sense of truly being in the presence of someone exceptional, and it made her feel special.

To narcissists, the façade is everything. Who they appear to be is who they believe they are. They are immersed wholly and completely in their fantasy of themselves. That is why they are so believable. Narcissists are preoccupied with their own delusions about their self-importance and superiority. They believe they are entitled to special treatment, and they work to make you believe it too. Some narcissists are very grandiose, and others are more quietly superior. They have an intense need to be perfect, well thought of, in control, and more significant than anyone else. You think you're being included in that top ranking, but you really aren't.

WHAT'S BELOW THE SURFACE?

Below the façade of charm, humor, beguiling attentiveness, boastful self-confidence, and stories of successes and accomplishments is a completely different person—one who is deeply selfish, needy, and controlling. The term "narcissism" is used to denote people who are at their core self-centered, self-absorbed, calculating, and manipulative. They hide and deny, even to themselves, these inner flaws while presenting a perfect image to the world. Only when you get really close to a narcissist will you find he's frequently defensive, angry, hostile, and demeaning.

Narcissists want desperately to form a relationship that will supply their endless need for attention and provide a scapegoat for their blame. They look for someone who will give in to their control, who will take care of their endless demands, and who will be deeply attached to them and put up with their needy self-centeredness.

As you've struggled to understand your relationship with a narcissist, you may have come across many different descriptions and explanations for their behaviors. Narcissists can have passive-aggressive traits; act obsessive and compulsive; be rageful; have drug, alcohol, sex, or gambling addictions; or be hypochondriacs. They enter relationships quickly and intensely, with lots of charm and attention on you, and when they're sure you are fully committed, they switch back to a complete focus on themselves, their wants and needs. Some are extremely emotionally destructive, and others can be more benevolent. Some need constant attention from you. Others pour themselves into benevolent projects with other people to get community attention and praise while ignoring you for weeks at a time.

Angela was smitten by Blake at first sight. He was witty, outrageous, and edgy. Within days they were living together, but it was several months before Angela realized that Blake had taken over her entire life—arranging all their social contacts; always deciding what restaurants, movies, and events to attend; and even choosing what Angela would wear. When she tried to make different choices, he would laugh, dismiss her ideas, and refuse to do much of anything her way. She found it easier to give in than to think about leaving the relationship.

In actuality, narcissists are two people in one body. The False Self protects and hides a repressed, vulnerable, negative, and despised inner self. This is called "splitting."[2] They have two very different parts of their personalities—a positive self and a disowned, hidden negative self. The closer contact you have with a narcissist, the more likely these two parts will get tangled up, and you'll see that hidden shadow self as he projects it onto you.

HOW CAN YOU TELL WHETHER A PERSON IS A NARCISSIST?

I use the duck test—that is, if it looks like a duck and quacks like a duck, it probably is a duck. There are no physical blood tests, MRIs, or exact determinations that can identify narcissism. Even therapists have to go on their observations of the behavior, attitudes, and reactions that a person presents to determine narcissism. So here are the symptoms and behaviors you should look for. Keep in mind that not all of these have to be present to make a determination of narcissism. According to the *Diagnostic and Statistical Manual*,[3] which therapists use as a guide, the person needs only 55 percent of the identified characteristics to be considered narcissistic. The list here is descriptive to give you a more real-life picture of the narcissist's common behaviors.

Superiority and Entitlement

The world of the narcissist is all about good/bad, superior/inferior, and right/wrong. There is a definite hierarchy, with the narcissist at the top—which is the only place he feels safe. Narcissists have to be the best, the most right, and the most competent; do everything their way; own everything; and control everyone. Interestingly enough, narcissists can also get that superior feeling by being the worst; the most wrong; or the most ill, upset, or injured for a period of time. Then they feel entitled to receive soothing concern and recompense, and even the right to hurt you or demand apologies to "make things even."

High Need for Attention and Validation

Narcissists need constant attention—even following you around the house, asking you to find things, or constantly saying something to grab your attention. Validation for a narcissist counts only if it comes from others. Even then, it doesn't count for much. A narcissist's need for validation is like a funnel. You pour in positive, supportive words, and they just flow out the other end and are gone. No matter how much you tell narcissists you love them, admire them, or approve of them, they never feel that it's enough—because deep down they don't believe anyone can love them. Despite all their self-absorbed, grandiose bragging, narcissists are actually very insecure and fearful of not measuring up. They constantly try to elicit praise and approval from others to shore up their fragile egos, but no matter how much they're given, they always want more.

Perfectionism

Narcissists have an extremely high need for everything to be perfect. They believe they should be perfect, you should be perfect, events should happen exactly as expected, and life should play out precisely as they envision it. This is an excruciatingly impossible demand, which results in the narcissist feeling dissatisfied and miserable much of the time. The demand for perfection leads the narcissist to complain and be constantly dissatisfied.

High Need for Control

Since narcissists are continually disappointed with the less than perfect way that life unfolds, they want to do as much as possible to control it to their liking. They want and demand to be in control, and their sense of entitlement makes it seem logical to them that they should be in control—of everything. Narcissists always have a story line in mind about what each "character" in their interaction should be saying and doing. When you don't behave as expected, they become quite upset and unsettled. They don't know what to expect next, because you're off script. They demand that you say and do exactly what they have in mind so they can reach their desired conclusion. You are a character in their internal play, not a real person with your own thoughts and feelings.

Lack of Responsibility—Blaming and Deflecting

Although narcissists want to be in control, they never want to be responsible for the results—unless, of course, everything goes exactly their way and their desired result occurs. When things don't go according to their plan or they feel criticized or less than perfect, the narcissist places all the blame and responsibility on you. It has to be someone else's fault. Sometimes that blame is generalized, for example, all police, all bosses, all teachers, all Democrats, and so on. At other times the narcissist picks a particular person or rule to blame, for example, his mother, the judge, or laws that limit what he wants to do. Most often, however, the narcissist blames the one person who is the most emotionally close, most attached, loyal, and loving in his life—you. To maintain the façade of perfection, narcissists always have to blame someone or something else. You are the safest person to blame, because you are least likely to leave or reject him.

Lack of Boundaries

Narcissists can't accurately see where they end and you begin. They are
a lot like two-year-olds. They believe that everything belongs to them,
everyone thinks and feels the same as they do, and everyone wants the
same things they do. They are shocked and highly insulted to be told
no. If a narcissist wants something from you, he'll go to great lengths to
figure out how to get it through persistence, cajoling, demanding, re-
jecting, or pouting.

Lack of Empathy

Narcissists have very little ability to empathize with others. They tend to
be selfish and self-involved and are usually unable to understand what
other people are feeling.[4] Narcissists expect others to think and feel the
same as they do and seldom give any thought to how others feel. They
are also rarely apologetic or feel remorseful or guilty.

However, narcissists are highly attuned to perceived threats, anger,
and rejection from others. At the same time, they are nearly blind to the
other feelings of the people around them. They frequently misread
subtle facial expressions and are typically biased toward interpreting
facial expressions as negative. Unless you are acting out your emotions
dramatically, the narcissist won't accurately perceive what you're feeling. Even saying "I'm sorry" or "I love you" when the narcissist is on
edge and angry can backfire. He won't believe you and may even mis-
perceive your comment as an attack. In addition, if your words and
expressions aren't congruent, the narcissist will likely respond errone-
ously. This is why narcissists often misinterpret sarcasm as actual agreement or joking from others as a personal attack. Their lack of ability to
correctly read body language is one reason narcissists are deficiently
empathetic to your feelings. They don't see them, they don't interpret
them correctly, and overall they don't believe you feel any differently
than they do.

Narcissists also lack an understanding about the nature of feelings.
They don't understand how their feelings occur. They think their feelings are *caused* by someone or something *outside* of themselves. They
don't realize that their feelings are caused by their own biochemistry,
thoughts, and interpretations. In a nutshell, narcissists always think *you*

cause their feelings—especially the negative ones. They conclude that because you didn't follow their plan or because you *made* them feel vulnerable, you are to blame.

This lack of empathy makes true relationships and emotional connection with narcissists difficult or impossible. They just don't notice what anyone else is feeling.

Emotional Reasoning

You've probably made the mistake of trying to "explain" and use logic with the narcissist to get him to understand the painful effect his behaviors have on you. You think that if he understands how much his behaviors hurt you, he'll quit doing them. Your explanations, however, don't make sense to the narcissist, who only seems able to be aware of his own thoughts and feelings. Although narcissists may say they understand, they honestly don't.

Therefore, narcissists make most of their decisions based on how *they* feel about something. They just have to have that red sports car, based entirely on how they feel driving it, not by whether it is a good choice to make for the family or for the budget. If they're bored or depressed, they want to move or end the relationship or start a new business. They always look to something or someone outside themselves to solve their feelings and needs. They expect you to go along with their "solutions," and they react with irritation and resentment if you don't.

Splitting

The narcissist's personality is split into good and bad parts, and they also split everything in their relationships into good and bad. Any negative thoughts or behaviors are blamed on you or others, whereas they take credit for everything that is positive and good. They deny their negative words and actions, while continually accusing you of being disapproving.

They also remember things as completely good and wonderful or as bad and horrible. They can't seem to mix these two constructs. Marty labeled the whole vacation ruined and the worst ever because the hotel room didn't meet his expectations and the weather wasn't perfect. Bob was blamed for twenty years because he wasn't there when his wife had their first child even though he was stranded in Chicago in a snowstorm. Marie's husband dismissed her concerns about the $30,000 cost for the new landscaping because he loved it. Narcissists aren't able to see, feel, or remember both the positive and the negative in a situation. They can deal with only one perspective at a time—theirs.

Fear

The narcissist's entire life is motivated and energized by fear. Most narcissists' fears are deeply buried and repressed. They're constantly afraid of being ridiculed, rejected, or just plain wrong. They may have fears about germs, about losing all their money, about being emotionally or physically attacked, about being seen as bad or inadequate, or about being abandoned. This makes it difficult and sometimes impossible for the narcissist to trust anyone else.

In fact, the closer your relationship becomes, the less he will trust you. Narcissists fear any true intimacy or vulnerability because they're afraid you'll see their imperfections and judge or reject them. No amount of reassurance seems to make any difference, because narcissists deeply hate and reject their own shameful imperfections. Narcissists never seem to develop trust in the love of others, and they continually test you with worse and worse behaviors to try to find your breaking point. Their gripping fear of being "found out" or abandoned never seems to dissipate.

Anxiety

Anxiety is an ongoing, vague feeling that something bad is happening or about to happen. Some narcissists show their anxiety by talking constantly about the doom that is about to happen, and some hide and repress their anxiety. But most narcissists project their anxiety onto their closest loved ones. They accuse you of being negative, unsupportive, mentally ill, not putting them first, not responding to their needs, or being selfish. All of this is designed to label you with their anxiety in an attempt to not feel it themselves. As you feel worse and worse, the narcissist feels better and better. In fact, he feels stronger and more superior as you feel your anxiety and depression grow.

Shame

Narcissists don't feel much guilt because they think they are always right, and they don't believe their behaviors really affect anyone else. However, they harbor a lot of shame. Shame is the belief that there is something deeply and permanently wrong or bad about who you are. Buried in a deeply repressed part of the narcissist are all the insecurities, fears, and rejected traits that he is constantly on guard to hide from everyone, including himself. The narcissist is acutely ashamed of all these rejected thoughts and feelings. For example, I had one narcissistic client who was into skydiving and other intense, risk-taking behaviors tell me that he never felt fear. "Fear," he said, "was evil." He was clearly on a crusade to defeat it.

Keeping his vulnerabilities hidden is essential to the narcissist's pretend self-esteem or False Self. Ultimately, however, this makes it impossible for them to be completely real and transparent.

Inability to Be Truly Intimate

Because of their inability to understand feelings, lack of empathy, and constant need for self-protection, narcissists can't truly love or connect emotionally with other people. They cannot look at the world from anyone else's perspective. They're essentially emotionally blind and alone. This makes them emotionally needy. When one relationship is no longer satisfying, they often overlap relationships or start a new one as soon as possible. They desperately want someone to feel their pain, to sympathize with them, and make everything just as they want it to be. However, they have little ability to respond to your pain or fear or even your day-to-day need for care and sympathy.

Can't Cooperate and Be a Team Member

Thoughtful, cooperative behaviors require a real understanding of each other's feelings. How will the other person feel? Will this action make both of us happy? How will this affect our relationship? These are questions that narcissists don't have the capacity or the motivation to think about. Don't expect the narcissist to understand your feelings, give in, or give up anything he wants for your benefit; it's useless.

WHAT ABOUT SOCIOPATHS?

Narcissists and sociopaths are not the same. It's often hard to tell the difference when you only look at outward behaviors. There's a big difference, however, when you look at their hidden vulnerabilities. Sociopaths pretty much have no emotional vulnerabilities. They are born without fear, anxiety, shame, guilt, or *any* empathy. They do not care about your feelings even a little. Narcissists, on the other hand, want to have a relationship, but they have some real disabilities in their capacity to respond with compassion and understanding.[5]

Sociopaths do not have any desire for a relationship with you. Their goal is to get whatever it is you have that they want—such as money, property, sex, attention, cooperation—without giving you anything in exchange and then move on. Narcissists often keep hanging on to the relationship with you even after you split up because they want that connection and continued attention.

If you're recovering from manipulation or abuse by a sociopath, you'll need more help than this book can provide. You have been severely abused, and you may need ongoing psychotherapy, deprogramming, or intensive emotional care. However, this book can lead you in the right direction toward increasing your self-esteem and becoming more self-loving.

CONCLUSION

For narcissists, life is all about *them*. They create an appealing and charming façade to hook you into a relationship, but hidden under that False Self are a multitude of relationship limitations and dysfunctional emotional responses. The narcissist promises to take care of you and make you the center of his life, only to turn the tables on you and demand that you be totally focused on him. Narcissists hide their emotional deficits or blame you for "making them" act angry, hurtful, and selfish. It's not until you are truly committed to the relationship that you discover how many discrepancies there are between the narcissist's presented image and his real personality.

You got hooked into this relationship under false pretenses. What you were offered and thought you were getting disappeared almost immediately after you made a commitment. It will never return for any length of time.

In the next chapter I'll share with you information about the qualities and relationship patterns that *you* brought to this relationship and how they mesh with the narcissist's characteristics.

QUESTIONS FOR REFLECTION

Which of the behaviors presented here does the narcissist in your life have?

What traits or behaviors attracted you to the narcissist? Which of those are still present on a daily basis now?

What effect has the narcissist's blame and anger had on you?

How has the narcissist's lack of empathy affected your relationship?

Can you identify times when the narcissist completely misread or misinterpreted things you said or did?

What traits of fear, anxiety, and shame have you seen in the narcissist?

What percentage of the behaviors mentioned in this chapter does the narcissist in your life exhibit?

2

WHAT ABOUT *YOU*?

"I thought I knew who I was, but I was you."
—Rumi

WHY THE NARCISSIST NEEDS YOU TO BE A CARETAKER

Narcissists are actually very needy, insecure, and emotionally disabled, so it is vital for them to be in a relationship with someone who can take care of all of these deficits. Narcissists are highly self-oriented, but they need a partner to help them project their illusion of competence and perfection in the world. Although they are emotional loners, they don't ever want to be alone.

They also want someone who will accept all of their cast-off feelings and still love, accept, and stay with them without their having to change. People who are willing to take on this role I call emotional caretakers.[1] If you have been in a relationship with a narcissist for any length of time, either you already were an emotional caretaker or you have since become one.

EMOTIONAL CARETAKERS—OTHER ORIENTED

People who become emotional caretakers to a narcissist tend to naturally be *highly* empathetic, agreeable, easygoing, and flexible. They're considerate, caring, generous, and giving. They look for the good in others, and they like to please others. They're steady and reliable and want to do a good job. When they see someone who needs help, they are often the first ones to step in. Giving to others gives them pleasure. They make excellent workers, staunch friends, loving parents, and loyal spouses. So far, this describes really nice, caring people.

However, to consistently be an emotional caretaker for a narcissist, you have to also have some self-defeating traits, otherwise you wouldn't have stayed in the relationship. Caretakers tend to be overly giving, overly loyal, and too empathetic—traits that narcissists highly encourage and use to their advantage. You probably have a strong sense of guilt even when something isn't your fault. You might have a hidden tendency toward low self-esteem and a fear of anger or disagreements, and you may be easily manipulated by blame, accusation, and disappointment from others. You probably discount your own wants and needs and give in too much to others. Caretakers usually downplay their own good qualities while admiring and praising the good in others—a narcissist's dream come true. And finally, you are probably not comfortable being in charge.

These strengths and susceptibilities make you a perfect match for what the narcissist needs. Let's look at these qualities in more depth.

STRENGTHS

Superempathetic

What narcissists lack in empathy, emotional caretakers make up for in overflowing measure. Caretakers are extremely empathetic—actually more along the lines of being sympathetic. That is, you may actually feel your loved ones' feelings more strongly than your own. You're extremely good at reading even the smallest facial cues and body language, and you often know what other people feel before they do. So the narcissist just has to "give that look," and you'll jump into action to take care of things. Obviously, this is very appealing to the narcissist, who already expects you to read his mind.

Agreeable, Easygoing, and Flexible

Emotional caretakers typically respond to requests from others with "OK, fine, sure, I'd be happy to do that." This doesn't necessarily mean you actually want to do what is being asked. It's likely that you don't even think about saying no. Caretakers try to be as agreeable and pleasing as possible. When plans change, you don't worry too much but are adaptable and flexible. You tend to be easygoing, so it doesn't feel difficult to adjust your preferences to meet those of the narcissist. In addition, when the narcissist is being rigid and upset about sudden changes and adjustments in plans, you easily smooth things over and move forward.

Generous and Giving

Emotional caretakers share easily, give generously, and automatically look for ways to help others. You get a lot of personal pleasure and satisfaction out of giving your time, attention, energy, and even money and other kinds of tangible help. You often don't even keep track of how much you're giving, nor do you expect others to give as much as you do. You just take it for granted that other people will reciprocate in kind when they are able. You often don't notice that the narcissist isn't giving you nearly as much or repaying your kindness until the balance sheet is extremely unequal.

Look for the Good in Others

Emotional caretakers don't like to speak negatively about anyone. You prefer to look for the smallest bit of goodness in others and focus entirely on that. You just expect that others will treat you as kindly and caringly as you would treat them. Caretakers are big believers in second chances, hope, willingness to change, and transformation. Narcissists find your tendency to be validating and optimistic very enjoyable. Even when the narcissist acts rude, hurtful, or selfish, you typically forgive and understand, hoping for better behavior in the future.

Steady and Reliable

Caretakers are reliable. You follow through, keep your promises, do more than your fair share, and can be counted on when things go awry. You're dependable, trustworthy, and consistent. You take the bad with the good and keep your focus on the solution. If there is a problem, you're ready to step in and work toward a resolution. You are not deterred by difficulties or complications. Caretakers like things to go smoothly and are willing to put in the effort to resolve things in a positive way.

Like to Please Others

Making others happy makes the caretaker happy. You're a peacemaker. You don't like to be around conflict and disagreement. You work to find compromise and develop cooperation. You're willing to acknowledge your mistakes and make amends. Most caretakers search for solutions that are mutually beneficial. As a result, it can be upsetting to you when the other person is angry, displeased, or dissatisfied and won't work to resolve an issue.

SUSCEPTIBILITIES AND VULNERABILITIES

Overly Loyal

Once an emotional caretaker makes a promise, it's forever. In adults, promises are usually reciprocal, in other words, I'll do this, and you'll do that or I'll give this, and you'll give that. This applies to many things, such as promises of love, friendship, marriage, financial support, or fidelity, and even small things like promises of going somewhere together, being somewhere on time, or even cleaning the kitchen. Caretakers are meticulous about keeping their promises but amazingly undemanding that other people keep their reciprocal promises. Even when the narcissist breaks all of his promises, you're likely to keep on as if everything in the relationship were just as it should be. You believe that if you keep your promises and stay loyal, the narcissist will eventually come around and fulfill his promises to you.

Overly Sympathetic

Emotional caretakers often have more sympathy for others than they have for themselves. For example, do you hate to disappoint others, be disliked, or have someone be upset with you for even a short time? You may chastise yourself for any anger, mistake, or hurt you cause others, but you easily forgive the narcissist for his self-oriented, rude, or hurtful behaviors.

This difference in how you treat yourself versus what you expect from the narcissist puts your relationship out of balance. By giving too much and expecting too little, you have set a standard that it's OK to discount or ignore your feelings, wants, and needs. Kind and healthy people see this and try not to impose on you too much. Narcissists zero in on you because this imbalance is exactly what they are looking for.

Overly Giving

Because you often forget about your own needs, you can become exhausted, irritated, and disappointed in others. Caretakers strongly believe in giving in order to receive. When you want love, caring, kindness, or consideration, your first thought is to give more of these things to others so they will give them to you. However, you may be *so* self-sufficient that you often don't ask for consideration or even give other people a chance to reciprocate.

With a narcissist, you eventually feel unappreciated and taken advantage of, and the relationship becomes more and more unbalanced. This overgiving makes you highly attractive to the narcissist, who greatly enjoys the comfort of this imbalance.

Strong Sense of Guilt: Never Good Enough

There may be another reason you overgive in relationships—you may feel that you aren't good enough so you *should* give more. Most caretakers expect themselves to meet extremely high standards of goodness, which can lead to feelings of guilt for not doing enough for others, not being kind enough, or not going the extra mile. This makes you easy prey for the narcissist's pattern of blaming others. Narcissists notice your feelings of guilt and inadequacy and use them to get what they want from you.

Fear of Anger and Disagreement

Emotional caretakers don't like anger, disagreements, or discord. They sometimes physically recoil from these negative situations and may even have a loathing reaction to conflict. When under stress, many caretakers freeze, can't think of what to say, and prefer to give in rather than fight. Caretakers frequently grow up in families where there was either a lot of dysfunctional conflict or no conflict at all, so you may not have learned effective conflict-resolution skills. You may not know how to effectively stand up for yourself or tolerate inharmonious environments.

When you're in a relationship with a narcissist, there are a lot of conflicts. The narcissist always wants to do things his way, so you must either give in all the time or fight for what you want. Narcissists use your fears about conflict to coerce, control, and force you to give them what they want. You can find it extremely hard to stand up to such an intimidating and stubborn person.

Weak Boundaries

A boundary is a line that separates you from someone else. Boundaries are like protective fences that guard your belongings, rights, privacy, and even individuality. Many boundaries are set by social convention or law, but most are set when you do things like say no, close a door, hang up the phone, or don't allow someone to treat you in a particular way. Boundaries, by definition, are a way to keep other people and their energy at a distance—even when they don't like it.

Setting boundaries when the other person doesn't want the separation can be quite a challenge for caretakers. You don't like being disagreeable or demanding. You also just expect others to follow convention and respect your boundaries, without your having to define or defend them.

When you get into a relationship with a narcissist, you're shocked and surprised that he doesn't recognize or honor your boundaries. In fact, narcissists don't see any difference between you and them, your feelings and theirs, your opinions and theirs, or your property and theirs. Their blindness to boundaries makes it imperative that you set boundaries over and over to keep your space and identity intact. This can be extremely exhausting and painful to do because the narcissist can be very persistent, while you are strongly uncomfortable with disagreements, conflict, and selfishness. You want others to be happy and agree to the boundaries you set. So all the narcissist has to do is disagree, and he's in control. If you don't feel it's right to take action until the narcissist agrees, you'll always lose.

Lance tried to set limits on how much Serena spent, but she would just open new credit card accounts and continue buying stuff. All the closets were full, and there were piles of things Serena had "bought on sale" that she had never even opened. Lance would pay off the credit cards and close them, only to have Serena find other ways to get money. He hated fighting and couldn't figure out an effective way to say no and have it honored.

Denial of Your Own Wants, Needs, and Feelings

Emotional caretakers are often so busy empathizing with other people's feelings and needs that they pay little or no attention to their own. By the time you're in need of emotional support, you've already set a pattern with the narcissist that he can discount and invalidate your feelings and opinions and get away with it. Narcissists already think your feelings are annoying and interfering in their fantasy scenario, so they work consistently to talk you out of what you feel and want. When the narcissist says you don't feel or want what you just said you feel and want, you are more likely than most people to go along with that distortion of reality and give in.

Disavowing Your Own Strengths

Humbleness can be a good quality. However, emotional caretakers tend to take their uniquely high levels of love, empathy, caring, cooperative spirit, and generosity for granted. This leads you to assume that you're average and that everyone else has the same abilities. It can be hard for you to comprehend or even believe that these same qualities are exceptionally low or missing for most narcissists. This lack of appreciation for your abilities can make you vulnerable to the devaluing that narcissists do to you in relationships.

Uncomfortable with Power

Many emotional caretakers think that being powerful is the same thing as being mean, uncaring, and controlling. Therefore, you can end up feeling uncomfortable and even embarrassed to exert power. If you grew up with either a controlling, narcissistic parent or in a home where there was always agreement, you may feel especially guilty for wanting anything to be your way, fighting for your autonomy, or using power to get your needs and wants met.

In reality, the power you need to embrace is the power over yourself and your choices. This includes the power to be who you are without apology, the power to live your life as you choose, the power to say no and yes, and the power to be in a safe, comfortable, and respectful environment. If you don't use your power to protect yourself, then the narcissist will always overwhelm you, leaving you vulnerable to his manipulation and control.

Narcissists like that you're so giving and easygoing. They put a lot of pressure on you to give up taking care of yourself and focus entirely on their wants and needs. When you focus so intently on someone else, you can end up losing yourself.

Marcie's mother was self-absorbed, controlling, and demanding. So when Marcie met Matt, she didn't even notice how much of the time Matt was in control of everything they did. She just enjoyed his charm, self-confidence, and prestige as a cardiac surgeon. Most of her attention was on her beautiful home and raising the children. After twenty years of marriage, she was shocked when Matt filed for divorce and married his twenty-eight-year-old office assistant. Marcie was at a loss at age forty-six to figure out what to do with the rest of her life. She had focused entirely on Matt's goals and choices, and now she was horrified to have that lifestyle taken away from her. She didn't even know what food she preferred, who her real friends were, or how to spend her evenings without Matt.

THE MAGNETIC ATTRACTION

Narcissists are easily attracted to people with caretaking qualities. As with any relationship, there needs to be a blend of similarities and differences. Ross Rosenberg, in his book *The Human Magnet Syndrome: Why We Love People Who Hurt Us*, says that the differences between narcissists and caretakers act as magnetic polar opposites that attract.[2] The qualities in each are enhanced or neutralized by the qualities in the other.

Narcissists and caretakers have many differences that pull them together. Narcissists want someone to look after them, and caretakers love to give and care for others. Narcissists like being in control and getting their own way, whereas you're more willing to give in to what they want. Narcissists are intense, confident, and decisive, whereas you're more easygoing, laid back, agreeable, and willing to let others be in charge. Narcissists are always coming up with something new, and you're good at transforming their ideas into concrete reality. Narcissists are distractible and spontaneous, whereas you're stable and reliable. You're extremely empathetic, which can disguise the narcissist's low empathy. Lastly, narcissists feel entitled to get whatever they want, whereas you will usually sacrifice your own wants and needs for the narcissist.

There are also some similarities connecting narcissists and caretakers. You both carry a hidden need to be perfect and a fear of being inadequate. However, the narcissist pretends to be perfect, while you work tirelessly to become perfect. Narcissists don't have boundaries, and you find it very hard to set boundaries. Narcissists and caretakers both dislike negativity. The narcissist, however, blames his negativity on you, whereas you work hard to change the narcissist into a more positive person. You are both strongly affected by fear. Yours is the fear of conflict and guilt, whereas the narcissist's is the fear of shame and humiliation. And you both have a deep need and desire to be committed, connected, and completely immersed in a relationship with another person.

These similarities and differences work like magnets to attract you to each other. Unfortunately, they also work to keep you from being truly intimate. Intimacy requires two people willing and able to be vulnerable, open, and emotionally close. You and the narcissist may have physical and sexual closeness, trying to do everything together, and even pretending to think and feel alike. But intimacy requires sharing your deepest differences and weaknesses and exposing your tender feelings. Narcissists can't risk that level of vulnerability, and they make it unsafe for you to risk it either. I'll explore this in the next chapter.

CONCLUSION

If you weren't a caretaker before you entered this relationship, it was inevitable that you would become one. The narcissist demands that you respond with caretaking behaviors, or he'll make life miserable. Narcissists inexorably push you more and more into focusing on them and less and less on yourself. They discount and disregard your feelings, thoughts, and needs, while demanding your full attention and compliance.

Being other oriented, caretakers bring high levels of empathy, flexibility, generosity, reliability, and caring for others to their relationships. These are wonderful traits, but they have to be balanced with boundaries, good self-care, and the ability to stand up for yourself. When you connected to the narcissist, your caretaking qualities actually made you highly susceptible to being used and taken advantage of by him. The narcissist kept you enmeshed and controlled, filling his needs by using your kindness, loyalty, and willingness to give in to meet his wishes. You had hoped the charming, fun part of the narcissist that you fell in love with would finally reappear if you were more perfect, compliant, and agreeable—but that rarely happened.

Strangely, it appears that the more of a caretaker you became, the more the narcissist pulled away, demanded more, and disdained your efforts. And now, after all you've given and put up with, the narcissist wants out and blames you for all of his dissatisfactions. It's so unfair.

QUESTIONS FOR REFLECTION

Which caretaker traits do you see in yourself?

What feelings, wants, and needs have you repressed or hidden in this relationship?

Which caretaker traits have made you vulnerable to manipulation by the narcissist?

How does the narcissist use your caretaker traits against you?

In what ways are you and the narcissist alike? How are you different?

Can you put into words what magnetically attracted you to the narcissist?

Do you act as a caretaker in any other relationships?

3

WHY RELATIONSHIPS WITH NARCISSISTS ARE ALWAYS DOOMED

"Anyone who wants you to live in misery for their happiness should not be in your life to begin with."
—Isaiah Hankel, author, speaker, and Fortune 500 consultant

Your relationship with the narcissist was always doomed. The most common ways relationships with narcissists end up are as follows: (1) The narcissist gets bored, feels too vulnerable, doesn't want to act more mature and caring, or feels humiliated—and leaves. (2) The caretaking partner gets fed up, and a final, unforgivable behavior by the narcissist triggers the caretaker to leave. (3) The caretaker becomes completely compliant, submissive, and dependent, and the narcissist leaves or just ignores the caretaker and creates a separate life. (4) Both the narcissist and the caretaker create independent, separate lives and continue to live together.

You'll notice that there is no scenario in which the narcissist changes into a loving, caring partner and you both live happily ever after. Narcissism is a serious personality disorder. It runs in families and seems to be increasing. This means that every narcissist is likely to have at least one primary relative with the disorder and that he was probably reinforced and rewarded for his narcissistic behavior growing up. By the time you meet and fall in love with the narcissist, he has had a lifetime of being who he is. Narcissists are no more likely to change their personalities than you are. In addition, narcissists almost always get everything they want either by persistence, charm, threat, or outright manipulation, so they're continually being rewarded to remain exactly who and what they are.

Hereditary traits and lifelong responses are not likely to change. To make any kind of change, the narcissist first has to admit that he has a serious problem and then put in continued, lifelong effort to act differently despite his natural urge to be narcissistic. He would have to learn ways to override his distorted perceptions and how to pretend to be empathetic and control his anger responses. That still leaves intact his belief that he is superior and his frantic need for attention to be dealt with. You can see the complexity and hugeness of the problem.

Should you give up hope of the narcissist's ever making any sort of change? What are the chances that the narcissist will "come to his senses"? When the narcissist says he's willing to change, can you have any expectation that it will happen? Will marital counseling help? How will the narcissist be as a parent after a divorce? There are so many questions and few answers, with only vague responses from the professionals.

WHAT IS UNLIKELY TO CHANGE

Lack of Empathy

All of the narcissist's empathy responses are impaired because the "empathy circuit" in his brain doesn't function properly.[1] Remember, narcissists can't clearly perceive and interpret other's feelings, and they don't understand or care a great deal how their behavior affects others. If you respond with hurt or anger to something the narcissist does, he will simply be baffled by your feelings, discount their authenticity, and even tell you that your feelings are wrong or stupid.

Simon Baron-Cohen shares his thirty years of research on empathy in his book *Zero Degrees of Empathy*.[2] He states that sociopaths have basically no empathy at all, and that narcissists have a minimal ability for empathy. He goes on to say that empathy is both a biological mechanism and a learned behavior. His research on the empathy circuit in the brain shows that it is affected by three things: neural circuitry that is inherited, the amount of stress or trauma a person has experienced, and short-term physical conditions, such as being tired, inebriated, or under pressure. Baron-Cohen has concluded that narcissists have permanent underactivity in their empathy circuit.

With intense training and motivation, the narcissist can learn to respond to others more empathetically. However, it doesn't appear to their family members that the narcissist *feels* more empathetic. He has just learned what to *say* and *do* more appropriately. In social situations, narcissists are pretty good at appearing to be caring. Nevertheless, in intimate relationships, where there is the greatest potential for deep emotional connection or intense conflict, the narcissist quickly reverts to self-centered reactions.

Merging

You can tell a narcissist that you feel different or you want something different than he does, but the narcissist rarely believes you. He just thinks that you are wrong, being stubborn, or mentally ill. Narcissists are convinced that you share their feelings, and they believe they're right, despite facts or information to the contrary. When you say you don't agree, the narcissist just thinks you are being obstinate. Since logical arguments seem to have no effect on the narcissist, the possibility for change in the narcissist is minimal.

Defensiveness and Self-Protection

You need to keep in mind that most narcissists see the world and other people as dangerous and out to expose and harm their vulnerable and hidden imperfections. That is why the False Self they portray to the world is so strong and, they hope, impenetrable. Threats of exposure of their inadequacies, deficiencies, flaws, or weaknesses will typically be met with blame, attack, criticism, denunciation, and projection of those flaws onto you. Having their vulnerabilities and imperfections exposed is devastating to their egos. This fear is so deeply rooted that it is nearly impossible to transform.

Lack of Caring

Narcissists can't seem to figure out what you feel, so they don't respond with much caring. Here's an example to show you how a narcissist perceives the world. Imagine that you are looking at a chair. What is the chair thinking? What is the chair feeling? What does the chair want? How would you treat a chair fairly? Sounds impossible to figure out, doesn't it? Since you assume that chairs don't have thoughts or feelings, you would never wonder about those questions.

You're the chair to the narcissist. See the problem? The narcissist doesn't see your feelings any better than you can see feelings in a chair. So he doesn't wonder about what you feel or want unless your reactions become a threat to what he wants. The rest of the time, the narcissist is mostly just thinking *How can I get what I want and keep this person from leaving?*

Unwilling to Share

Narcissists don't share. They think everything belongs to them. They're surprised that you would get upset when they take what they want. It appears that narcissists think that allowing you to be around them is sharing enough. They don't share their deepest feelings and true inner thoughts either, so intimacy doesn't naturally develop. Attempts to reach these inner feelings are usually met with stonewalling, avoidance, and outright anger and defensiveness.

Narcissists Don't Seek Help

Narcissists could have a chance to learn better ways to interact in relationships, but they are the least likely group to seek help. Narcissists rarely go into therapy. They keep their False Self intact by buying wholeheartedly into the fantasy that everyone else has a problem but they are perfectly fine. The rest of their family members may all be on medication or in therapy because of the narcissist's behaviors, but getting the narcissist into therapy is nearly impossible. Narcissists who grudgingly agree to go to therapy usually leave after a session or two or have an agenda to prove to the therapist that you're the crazy person. Unfortunately, they're frequently convincing, since many therapists without training in personality disorders can be charmed and tricked by the narcissist's confidence and self-assurance. Working with personality disorders is a highly specialized field, and most therapists have little or no training to work effectively with narcissists nor the understanding or awareness to identify the disorder.

If the narcissist finally does go to therapy with you and the therapist is knowledgeable, the likely progression will be as follows:

- Session one, the narcissist does everything possible to charm the therapist and paint you as irrational and hostile. You become angry and defensive.
- Session two, the narcissist becomes argumentative and pouting. You become stronger and start exposing some of the more hidden behaviors of the narcissist, such as sexual affairs, misuse of money, hostile words and behaviors, or even physical abuse.
- Session three, the narcissist doesn't show up or explodes in anger in the session and walks out, never to return.

Narcissism is a deeply embedded personality configuration that is tenacious and persistent and not easily amenable to change.

NARCISSIST/CARETAKER RELATIONSHIP PATTERNS

It is also hard to change the interaction patterns that develop between narcissists and caretakers. Narcissists don't understand caretakers, but neither do caretakers understand narcissists. As a highly empathetic caretaker, it's hard for you to even imagine what it would feel like *not* to be automatically compassionate, sympathetic, or considerate. Half of the time narcissists have no idea what you're talking about when you mention caring, trust, partnership, or intimacy. As you can see by now, these words mean entirely different things to the narcissist than to you. These basic miscommunications are nearly impossible to overcome because they are deeply embedded and hardwired in each of you.

When you try to talk about things, your words seem to indicate the same goals and needs, and you think that progress is being made. However, you and the narcissist mean entirely different things using the same words, and your internal emotional reactions are quite different.

Narcissists and caretakers can get into destructive patterns that reinforce each other's worst traits.

Pursuing and Distancing

Caretakers are pursuers, and narcissists are distancers. The more you reach out to the narcissist and ask him to share feelings, talk about the relationship, or discuss your differences, the more the narcissist backs away and gets defensive. The narcissist came on so strong at the beginning of the relationship that you got the impression he truly wanted to be close and intimate. Narcissists press hard for a quick commitment at the beginning of a relationship to seal the deal. Then they can relax without fear of abandonment and be themselves—totally self-absorbed and self-focused. Narcissists will give you just enough attention and cooperation to keep the relationship in place. When you ask for more than that minimal amount, they'll get angry or withdraw.

On the other hand, caretakers thrive on giving, sharing, and communicating about everything. When you sense moodiness in the narcissist, you immediately want to talk about it, fix it, and make your partner happy again. It's mystifying to you why the narcissist would get angry about that. His anger makes you want to talk things through even more and get things back on track, whereas the narcissist just wants to bury it and move on. Narcissists think all that talking is your way of trying to change them, and they know they don't want to change. They're already doing things the way they want to.

Fight, Flight, and Freeze

Most of us know about the fight or flight response, but there is another response that is part of that pattern—it's freeze.[3] Narcissists prefer to flee when they feel danger, but if cornered they'll fight. Caretakers more often freeze. That puts you at a huge disadvantage when dealing with a narcissist. When you freeze, your whole body and brain start shutting down. Your heart rate falls, your ability to think diminishes, and your breathing nearly stops. In the meantime, the narcissist is either out the door or verbally berating you. Fight, flight, and freeze are all fear responses, which are biologically based and designed to deal with attacking lions or natural disasters. When both parties have high levels of fear and anxiety, these automatic reactions can make it difficult to solve differences in intimate relationships. Adrenaline gets activated, and the ability to think and problem solve goes out the window.

To solve relationship problems, human beings need to feel safe, secure, and confident in the other person's love and commitment. They also need a sense of ease, trust, and understanding. The automatic fear reactions that you and the narcissist trigger in each other illustrate a core fact of the narcissist/caretaker relationship: *There is not enough trust and belief in the strength of the intimate bond to directly and fearlessly confront and overcome differences.* Somewhere, deep down, you both know this relationship works only one way—the way the narcissist wants it to work.

Parent and Child—Superior/Inferior

Narcissists always think and behave in a one-up and one-down pattern in their interactions with you. They need to be superior and right about everything. They also find most mundane chores beneath them or too much of a bother, so they expect you to do them and treat you like an underling. Narcissists want to put their energy into doing only the things they like to do. You end up taking up the slack, whether it's doing all the cooking, cleaning, family scheduling, or getting children to their activities. As the caretaker, you come to feel like the parent because the narcissist acts like a child who needs lots of caring and monitoring. The narcissist believes he's the boss and you're the subordinate, whereas you think of him as an obstinate child.

You both end up feeling superior and inferior at the same time. Instead of a team that works together for the benefit of all, you end up being in competition for who does the most work, who brings in the most money, who is irresponsible or selfish. Obviously, this works to create a rivalry rather than a partnership. It doesn't take long for this rivalry to spawn resentment that makes it nearly impossible to cooperate.

Persecutor, Victim, and Rescuer

The contentiousness in your relationship with the narcissist creates what is known as the "drama triangle," each of you alternately playing the persecutor, victim, or rescuer.[4] It goes like this: The narcissist acts as the persecutor when he blames you. You see this as unfair and feel like a victim. This goes on for a while, until you turn the tables and start blaming him, thus becoming the persecutor. The narcissist then becomes the victim. Or instead, you try to please and appease the narcissist by being the rescuer. In the rescuer role you try to get the narcissist to see things logically, or you make attempts to get the narcissist to change and act more caring and agreeable. This can quickly deteriorate into you demanding and persecuting and the narcissist feeling like a victim again. Narcissists hate that feeling, so they'll return to persecuting and push you back into being the victim. For a more in-depth description of this relationship dynamic, see chapter 2 in my book *Stop Caretaking the Borderline or Narcissist*.[5] Here is an example:

> Jim: "What do you mean there isn't enough money in the account? I told you I was going to buy those new golf clubs today." (Persecutor)
> Cayley: "I'm so sorry, but it's not my fault that the washing machine broke down, and then I had to get the kids' school supplies." (Victim)
> Jim: "You don't need to do all that right now. I need to get these clubs for the game on Saturday. The kids' stuff can wait, and you have plenty of clothes. The washer didn't need fixing until next month." (Persecutor)
> Cayley: "The kids start school this week. What was I supposed to do?" (Victim) "You're just being selfish. What's wrong with you?" (Persecutor)
> Jim: "Don't I have any rights around here? Everyone gets what they want, and nobody cares how I feel about anything." (Victim)
> Cayley: "Of course I care about you. I do everything you ask. I've been saving some money for a winter coat. I guess you could have that, but I just wish you would deal with this calmly instead of blowing up." (Victim, Rescuer, and then mild Persecutor)
> Jim: "What? You were hiding that money from me? You're really a greedy bitch." (Persecutor)
> Cayley: "Don't talk to me like that. You're really being mean. I just offered to help." (Rescuer) "You never appreciate anything I do." (Persecutor)

This pattern can go on and on, because there are only these three rather distasteful and ineffective roles to choose from. It becomes even more destructive when either one of you pulls in a child to play the third role.

As long as you are both involved in this triangular interaction, your relationship will always be in conflict and end in a standoff. However, every time you try to move out of this rigid pattern, the narcissist will do everything possible to pull you back in, because this is the only communication model that fits the narcissist's superior/inferior construct. It may also be extremely hard for you to "give up" the game, because it feels like the narcissist is "winning."

CARETAKER EXPECTATIONS THAT NARCISSISTS CAN'T MEET

Reciprocity

It's normal to have expectations for what you want in a relationship. You expect to do certain things for the other person, and you want him to do things that please, help, and support you. This is called reciprocity. This exchange is normal, and all ongoing relationships rely on this exchange of physical and emotional assistance. Everyone has his or her own unique hopes, dreams, and assumptions about how the relationship will develop.

Relationships between narcissists and caretakers have some significant imbalances in these expectations. Narcissists are almost entirely focused on what they will get out of the relationship, and caretakers are too focused on what they will give. Even so, the few things that you want, hope, and expect will always seem too difficult and burdensome to a narcissist.

Emotional Support

Caretakers commonly say they want a partner who will give emotional support. Caretakers often don't need a lot of support because they get such good feelings from giving to others, but they definitely need love, caring, thoughtfulness, validation, and reassurance—at least sometimes. Unfortunately, when they need support is typically the time the narcissist flees or wants to be given support—again.

Since narcissists are so self-absorbed, their support is rather random. However, random reinforcement is extremely powerful (for example, think of slot machine payouts). It eventually becomes difficult for care-takers to leave even when so little is gained because the next big payout may be just around the corner.

A client of mine said she felt that she got little support from her husband and was always asking for affection and consideration. She stayed in the relationship and kept surviving on his small tokens of caring until she ran across his will one day. As she read it, she saw that he had cut her out entirely—leaving the house, car, and all his savings to his daughter from his former marriage. If he died, she would be destitute. That was the last straw, but the signs had been there for years. She had tried to pretend that he loved her, but being left impoverished was the insult that she could see clearly.

Partnership

Most people today want a marriage that has a sense of teamwork or partnership. This requires that both parties identify their strengths and weaknesses and step in to help each other to accomplish their goals. Healthy relationships are built on this mutual assistance, which helps the entire family reach their common goals.

Narcissists, however, believe they are working alone to reach their goals. When a relationship ends, this egocentrism is more visible. You may have thought you were working together, but during a divorce you hear things such as "All you did was take care of the kids; I made all the money. Why should I just give it to you?" or "You need to move out, now. This house is mine," or "You better pay up big time for all the hurt and selfishness I had to put up with." You become the enemy. There is, and never was, any real sense of partnership other than in your fanta-sies.

Acceptance

When you met the narcissist, you felt completely accepted and adored. Once you became fully devoted and committed to the relationship, however, that feeling dwindled. The narcissist always wants and expects more, continually demanding that you prove you're good enough, car-ing, or thoughtful enough to be considered satisfactory. It's nearly impossible to feel true approval and acceptance. Without a reliable sense of acceptance, it's impossible for you to feel trusting and secure.

Intimacy

The thing caretakers say they want most from their partners is emotional intimacy. This usually refers to a feeling of exclusive closeness, deep knowledge and information about each other, special shared experiences, secret confidences, and sexual fidelity. Narcissists have a hard time doing any of these things exclusively and consistently. You think you're hearing special confidences, but many times things they tell you aren't even true because narcissists frequently lie or embellish their experiences and accomplishments to impress others.

I've had clients who found out years later that their spouses had been previously married and had children, or didn't finish their college degrees, or were never in the military, or had had affairs for over a decade. These are shocking revelations that can destroy any sense of trust and intimate closeness you may have thought you had.

For narcissists, intimacy primarily means sex. Sex fulfills their notion of closeness, without having to reveal anything about their vulnerabilities, inadequacies, faults, or mistakes. They feel reassured, without being emotionally exposed, and they often use sex to keep their partners securely attached.

What Does This Mean?

You have a right to expect your primary love relationship to fulfill basic emotional needs. Narcissists are great at telling you all the things they'll do for you when the relationship begins, but they just aren't able to meet anyone else's ongoing needs for any length of time. They find it challenging to consistently pay attention to any one person. They have just too many things about themselves that they have to think about. The narcissist's inability to meet your expectations is surely disappointing. You may occasionally get some of what you want, but it's not consistent and is often given grudgingly. So you're often disappointed and confused.

NARCISSIST'S EXPECTATIONS THAT CAN'T BE MET

Constant Attention

Narcissists love being in relationships because it gives them a 24/7 audience. You're expected to be available any time, day or night, give them all your attention, and not be distracted anywhere else—whether it is time spent at work, on the phone with your family, or even attending to your children's needs. The narcissist always wants to come first, be able to tap into your energy, and be noticed by you at any moment. He will barge in when the door is closed, follow you around the house, and ask you to fix things or handle a problem he has, always assuming you're available.

Even if you oblige and give all of your free time to the narcissist, he will typically not be satisfied. He may try to cut you off from your family and friends, convince you to work from home, or quit work altogether so you can be with him. Despite all that you give, the narcissist will still accuse you of being selfish and disloyal and not loving enough.

Adoration

Narcissists require total acceptance, recognition, approval, and agreement for everything they do, think, say, or want. They expect you to join their fantasy of being the greatest, most important, most knowledgeable, and most wonderful and perfect person of all time. The moment you no longer believe this fantasy, the narcissist will sense you pulling back and will go into overdrive to convince you to rejoin the illusion. If you can't regain your old enthusiasm, the narcissist moves into full harassment, criticism, and condemnation of your inadequacies, disloyalty, and selfishness.

Narcissists cannot live without this adoration. Unfortunately, no one can give them all the glorification and devotion they feel they deserve. So they are always on the lookout for more admiration by giving to their community, neighbors, or social groups, while ignoring the needs of their own family; quitting the job that supports the family to take off for a two-month cross-country bike ride, including blogs to admiring friends; having an affair; or spending evenings socializing with friends and ignoring you. These behaviors give the narcissist the admiration he craves while also punishing you for having needs and not giving him all that he wants.

Excitement

Narcissists are always looking for something new and exciting. One of my clients said that her husband had filled their garage with so many different types of sports equipment that they couldn't park their car in the garage. He had been completely enthusiastic about biking, skiing, tennis, and weight lifting, and he bought every piece of equipment and clothing for each sport. However, his interest in each had lasted less than six months before he moved on to something else. Narcissists often move from job to job, friend to friend, or relationship to relationship, always looking for the next big thing.

The narcissist also moves on to escape others from finding out that he isn't as advertised. Narcissists cancel activities with friends when they find something more "fun" to do. They "forget" their promises and commitments. They get easily insulted and feel rejected when others aren't instantly ready and excited to do what they want to do. They lose jobs when they don't follow through. Their quest for the new, the better, and the more exciting is a way of avoiding commitments, responsibilities, and imminent rejection.

Keeping Up the Façade

The narcissist expects you to keep the secret of his hidden, negative self. He may not ask you directly to keep his lapses and acting-out behaviors confidential, but it's implied or embedded in the narcissist's rule of "privacy." He says, "This is just between us. This is not something your family needs to know about," or he gives you that look, which says "This is not to be shared with others." This secret keeping cuts you off from the support of friends and family by involving you in a collusion about your relationship that ultimately makes it hard for you to be open and honest about your own life and emotional distress.

Any exposure on your part is treated as an enormous breach to the relationship. One client shared her hurt and disappointment about her marriage in an e-mail to John, an old high school boyfriend whom she hadn't seen in years. She wasn't allowed by the narcissist to talk with her family and friends about "personal" things. She had no romantic feelings for John but needed someone to help her understand her confusion and worry. When her narcissistic husband found out, he accused her of infidelity and filed for divorce. Sharing his inadequacies was an enormous betrayal to him.

Total Control

Narcissists want total control of everything that goes on in the relationship. He may expect to be in control of the money, the style and location of the house, and the type of discipline used with the children. He wants control over how you dress, what you eat, how much you exercise, how often you see your family, who your friends are, and where you vacation. Life is all about saving face and fear of exposure for the narcissist.

What Does This Mean?

The narcissist's expectations are so extreme and excessive that literally no one can ever hope to meet them. In addition, narcissists never seem to feel satisfied, no matter how much others do for them. They look for people with caretaking traits because they know caretakers will try the hardest to meet their expectations. These relationships last longer than other pairings for narcissists because caretakers are more willing to keep trying to meet their demands and expectations. Caretakers keep hoping that if they do everything right, narcissists will eventually keep their promises, but that never happens for long.

CONCLUSION

The information in these first three chapters is meant to show you why this relationship has not worked out the way you thought, hoped, and dreamed it would. It probably confirms what you feel, but may not have seen clearly, and clarifies why this relationship has been so complicated, mystifying, disappointing, and frustrating.

QUESTIONS FOR REFLECTION

What behaviors in the narcissist have you been hoping will change?

How much change in these behaviors have you seen over the course of your relationship?

What patterns between you and the narcissist have you been caught up in?

What part have you played in keeping these patterns going?

Which role do you most often take: victim, rescuer, or persecutor?

Make a list of the expectations you most want from an intimate relationship. Which of these did the narcissist fulfill?

What impossible demands has the narcissist made on you?

What do you think is likely to happen next in this relationship?

II

How Could This Be Over?

4

THE END GAME

"New beginnings are often disguised as painful endings."
—Lau Tzu

You are probably reading this book because your relationship with a narcissist is ending or has ended. This chapter looks at *how* these relationships end. Narcissists typically end the relationship, whereas caretakers are more likely to keep trying to make things work. You're more likely to keep hoping that things will improve. And you're the one more likely to seek out therapy to work on the relationship—even without the narcissist.

The question of why narcissists act the way they do was covered in the first three chapters. Now the questions are why does the narcissist want to end this relationship and should I agree to ending things? This chapter addresses these two questions.

WHY NARCISSISTS END RELATIONSHIPS

Narcissists end relationships for numerous reasons—boredom, not getting their insatiable needs met, someone or something else pulls their attention away, they want to be in romance again, they think you are causing their discontent, they don't like being responsible to you or for you, they want a new adventure, or they just want to start over. Deeper, more psychological reasons include that you know too much about their shortcomings, they feel inferior and inadequate around you, they're depressed and want to be admired and seen as perfect again, or they're just feeling old.

It's Not About You

You may notice that none of these reasons have much to do with you. They all have to do with how the narcissist interprets and reacts to his own feelings. Narcissists can't stand feeling anxious, fearful, despondent, or depressed. They become quickly desperate to feel better. Common reactions narcissists have when things aren't going well for them include getting angry, spending money, having more sex, getting overinvolved in a new project, or if all else fails, making a dramatic turnaround change in their own lives, such as changing jobs, moving, getting a divorce, having an affair, or changing their religion. If the narcissist is desperate to feel better, he may do all of these things at the same time.

It's Not Your Fault How the Narcissist Feels

Spending a lot of time trying to figure out what *you* did to make the narcissist pull away or end the relationship is not productive because it is extremely unlikely that you did anything out of the ordinary. Narcissists definitely like to blame you—and others—for things not going the way they want. It's important to remember that you don't actually *make* the narcissist feel or do anything. The narcissist may feel uncomfortable, dissatisfied, unhappy, and so on, but these feelings are inside of him and not under your direct control. The way you do things, say things, feel, or react may be perfectly acceptable or even delightful to someone else. The narcissist just sees you and the world from a skewed perspective. Narcissists have a delusional belief that their feelings are *caused* by the things that happen to them and the people around them.

The total change in the narcissist's demeanor, attitudes, and behaviors toward you since the breakup can be heartbreaking. How could anyone change so quickly and so completely? You went from being the closest of confidants to being the enemy for "no apparent reason." You may be trying to figure out what "caused" this change, but it is hard to put your finger on anything that you did that would be so awful or horrible. And you're right. You didn't do anything terrible. This change in your standing with the narcissist is completely within the mind-set of the narcissist. He may blame you for various and sundry missteps, but any healthy, loving person would be willing to work out these differences.

The narcissist latches on to anything to use as an excuse to "explain" his decision to reject and abandon you. Often, what the narcissist says is the problem is not the real reason.

Years ago one narcissistic client said she wanted to end her marriage because her husband was "uncouth." When I asked her how he was uncouth, she explained that he consistently went to important social functions with his shoes and belt not matching. As we kept talking I found out that her husband wanted his sixteen-year-old son to move in with them, which she was actually furious about but didn't want him to know because she would look bad.

Another narcissistic client was enraged and wanted out of the marriage because he felt his new four-year-old stepdaughter was disrespectful to him when she wouldn't clean her room. What he actually didn't like was that his wife gave the daughter more attention than she gave him.

In fact, events that happen are only one of several components that affect how we feel. Our interpretations, support system, and resources are also powerful factors. Narcissists are highly biased and skewed in their thinking, so they consistently and mistakenly interpret negative feelings as caused by outside events and other people. Narcissists also have a limited support system made up of one or two friends chosen to exactly reflect their views and thoughts. Therefore, these friends can't offer meaningful help or insight in difficult situations. The only resources that narcissists value and can count on are money and freedom. This leads them to consider divorce more easily. Many narcissists believe that divorce represents total freedom and complete control of all the money and all the decisions.

You Can't Fix Them

As a caretaker, you flew to make things better for the narcissist, even if you had to take the blame for something you didn't do. You may have tried to smooth things over, change how and what you said, and meet more of the narcissist's expectations. However, in the long run the narcissist always does what he *wants* to do. You can't change or control him. Trying to explain and get him to understand how you feel or to follow your suggestions leads to a lot of disappointment. Narcissists can't understand or relate to your feelings, and their interpretation of events will hardly ever match yours. Your words don't make sense to them. They may try to understand or pretend to understand, but in the long run you are talking two different languages. When it comes to understanding your feelings or motivations, the narcissist is blind and deaf.

WHEN NARCISSISTS LEAVE

When the relationship is at an end for the narcissist, it may come suddenly or may be long and drawn out. In either case, the narcissist has been stewing and probably discontented for some time without your ever knowing it. For narcissists, relationships always feel like an inner conflict and tension between freedom and abandonment, control and acquiescence, loneliness and suffocation. Their primary commitment is to their own survival, comfort, and safety.

Essentially, the narcissist will give just enough of whatever it is that you absolutely need to keep you in the relationship while also allowing him a satisfactory level of control, dominance, and freedom. That can be a tricky balance, and it can change from hour to hour and day to day. Whenever you try to make the relationship more to your liking, the narcissist will inevitably resist. However, he can sense that if he pulls too far away or gets too hostile or domineering, you may get upset enough to leave.

In actuality, the relationship between most caretakers and narcissists is not ideal for either of you. The narcissist wants a partner who is submissive and yet independent emotionally—an impossible ideal. Caretakers consistently say they want a relationship that is cooperative, accepting, and emotionally intimate and feels safe and comfortable. It is highly doubtful that the narcissist has met those criteria more than briefly after the first few days or months of the relationship.

Even so, relationships between narcissists and caretakers can sometimes last for years if a certain balance is found. Most relationships with narcissists, however, are fairly brief. Relationships are not static. Both parties change over the years, and narcissists don't deal well with changes that are out of their control. Children are born, both partners get older, jobs and roles change, interests evolve, willingness to tolerate disagreeable behaviors declines, and interest in particular friends and activities fades and changes. Each of these changes requires a rebalancing of the relationship, which is likely to cause conflict. Conflict with a narcissist requires the partner to give in or stand one's ground and suffer the consequences of his anger and hostility and at least temporary denunciation. Either party can get fed up with this pattern. As the pursuer, caretakers are more likely to want to "work things out," whereas the narcissist, being the distancer, is more inclined to leave.

Any significant change in you can also spell the end of the relationship. Some examples that clients have shared with me over the years include getting a long-term illness, such as fibromyalgia, cancer, depression, or increasing loss of eyesight or hearing; personal achievements, such as graduating from college, starting a new business or getting an award; entering the workforce; or changing your fight style, such as setting boundaries, speaking up more effectively about what you want, or refusing to be intimidated.

Changes in the narcissist's life can also lead to the end of the relationship. Examples include the narcissist's most hated or loved parent dies, severe illness or injury in which the narcissist can't function for a period of time, a midlife crisis, the narcissist's fear of getting old, a significant job promotion or demotion, or a huge weight loss or weight gain.

In healthy relationships life changes can be a challenge, but they tend to strengthen the relationship. Narcissists frequently see such changes as nullifying the underlying relationship commitment and agreement. This provides an opening for him to exit rather than contend with the difficulties of readjustment and growth.

Marjorie and Clay did pretty well in the first ten years of their relationship. Clay had a high-paying job in pharmaceutical sales. He thrived on hobnobbing with the medical doctors, going on trips paid for by his employer, having a million-dollar home, and generally feeling important and successful. Marjorie enjoyed her job as a teacher and spent a lot of time with their two children.

When the industry changed, Clay no longer got all those perks. His territory enlarged, but his commissions went down. Eventually he was laid off, replaced by computer-generated sales. He collapsed into a depression that lasted three years. They lost their house and had to rely entirely on Marjorie's teaching salary. Although they were getting by, Clay couldn't overcome the humiliation. He had to take a low-paying sales job. He met a young woman at work, and his affair with her pulled him out of his depression. It also demolished his marriage and family. Marjorie wanted to keep working on their life together, but Clay was off in a new direction and never looked back.

Narcissists find it hard to be without a relationship at all, so the timing or reason for their leaving is often based on their opportunity to move into another relationship quickly. Many narcissists already have a new partner picked out or have already started an affair before they leave. They literally can't stand to be out of enmeshment with someone for long.

HOW NARCISSISTS LEAVE: YOU HAVE TO BE THE BAD GUY

Push Away/Pull Back

Sometimes the relationship with a narcissist will end suddenly, with an entire cutoff. However, it is more likely that the narcissist will leave, then want to come back, reconnect, and reject you again—maybe several times. He says he never wants to hear from you again, but then he calls or sends e-mail messages that are infuriating and meant to reengage you. He wants a divorce but then agrees to go to therapy, which gives you hope. Then he quits therapy or doesn't show up. You never know where you stand.

If you don't want the relationship to end, these tactics keep you on edge—hopeful and yet frustrated. You feel pushed away, rejected, and disregarded, and then your hope is revived when he seems to be changing. However, if you don't come running back, he'll try to reengage you with unfair put-downs, false accusations, and biased remarks to others, which you probably feel you have to defend. Defensiveness and anger can keep you tied into the relationship even though nothing is improving.

This push away/pull back keeps you off balance and continually hoping for reconciliation. It can waste days, months, and even years of your life. Waiting for the narcissist to decide the fate of your relationship puts all the control in his hands. This is what narcissists prefer. They want to keep you around while they decide for sure what works the best for them or until they find a new partner. It is important for you to start making decisions about what you want to do.

They Try to Make You Leave First

Narcissists always want to be seen as blameless when their relationships end. One way to do this is to try to make you leave them. They go through a phase of devaluing you and putting you down. They make spiteful, cutting, and wounding comments. They blatantly don't keep their commitments—passively-aggressively "forgetting" or just rudely ignoring you. They refuse to tell you where they're going and who they're with. They say or do bizarre things while acting as if what they are doing is perfectly normal and appropriate. They accuse you of thoughts and behaviors that are not true, which leaves you feeling like you're the crazy one. This keeps them feeling righteous, and it keeps you furious and still engaged.

They Make Choices They Know You Will Reject

Another way the narcissist makes you the bad guy is to make a life choice that he knows you will reject. Some examples include a choice to move to another country, accepting a job that pays half of his current salary, or buying a house in another state without consulting you. When you get upset with these choices, you're accused of being unsupportive. If you agree to go along with these choices, he still isn't satisfied and may even increase his devaluing and criticisms of you, because he really just wanted you to leave.

More desperate attempts to push you out of the relationship can include bizarre and aggressive behaviors, such as getting another woman pregnant, moving a lover into the house you share, leaving on vacation alone and not returning, or selling a business and gambling the money away.

Sudden Trigger Event

Sometimes a triggering event will motivate the narcissist to leave. These are usually life-altering events for one of you. If you become ill or incapacitated or unable or unwilling to participate in the life the narcissist has designed, that may prompt the narcissist to leave. Even a positive event, such as having a child, can upset the delicate balance of the relationship, especially if it requires the narcissist to be more responsible and emotionally involved. Illnesses, aging, and job losses or promotions can act as triggers for the narcissist to suddenly abandon the relationship.

Blame

When things don't work out, the narcissist puts the blame entirely on someone else. You were on a pedestal at the beginning of the relationship. You were wonderful and perfect, and the narcissist was thrilled to have "won" you as a mate. Now that the narcissist sees the relationship as broken, damaged, and ending, now it's all your fault. He says you're too fat or too needy or too happy. You have wrecked things, destroyed the trust, ruined the best thing you ever had, crushed his love. You're unappreciative of all he has done for you. You would be nothing without him. You have single-handedly destroyed all the two of you have built. You're selfish and demanding. Overnight you have become the most despised person in the narcissist's life.

Obviously that is shocking, hurtful, insulting, and thoroughly unfair and wrong. When the narcissist reaches this point, he will no longer listen to you or give you any consideration and may no longer be willing to even speak to you. If you apologize profusely enough and beg for reconciliation, you may get back together for a while, but things between you will probably never be good again.

WHY IT'S HARD TO LEAVE A NARCISSIST

Your super loyalty, compassion, and desire to be true to your promises make it hard for you to consider leaving the relationship. The narcissist can also make it hard for you to leave because he wants to be in control of the decision to end the relationship. As long as keeping the relationship is the most important factor to you, the narcissist has free rein to dominate you and your decisions.

Caretakers are most likely to leave when the narcissist crosses a line that they finally can't or won't tolerate. But over the years, I have found it hard to predict when a caretaker will leave. The client whose narcissistic husband suffered a stroke and became physically abusive didn't leave. However, the client whose husband moved his pregnant girlfriend into the spare bedroom, saying she was an old friend from college down on her luck, did file for divorce. Caretaking men seem less likely to leave than women, perhaps because of the extra burden of responsibility that men culturally feel to take care of women.

When caretakers do leave, they find it is difficult to stick with their decision due to feelings of guilt or pity for the narcissist. And if the narcissist doesn't want you to leave, he'll keep pressuring you to change your mind, often with those same old promises to change. The narcissist can make your life extremely arduous, to keep control of you and the relationship.

You've Made a Mistake

After years of being told you are wrong and having your decisions devalued by the narcissist, you are probably prone to second-guessing yourself. And the narcissist will certainly try to convince you that you've made a mistake. He tries charisma, coaxing, persuasion, and then intimidation, goading, and outright provocation to get back in control of the relationship.

The narcissist will say "You just misinterpreted what I said. Of course, you should know that deep down I love you; why do I have to say it all the time? What about all the good times we've had together? You look at the negative too much. You don't understand the stress I've been under lately. You take things too personally. You're overreacting. You're too emotional."

Although the narcissist tries to sound positive about the relationship and why you shouldn't leave, you'll notice that all these "reasons" are actually negative remarks about you and what is wrong with what you're doing. These are not real encouragements to stay in the relationship;

they are actually manipulations to lower your self-esteem so you won't leave.

If the coaxing and persuasion don't work, the narcissist can bring out the especially negative evaluations to trigger your sore spots and make you feel bad about yourself: "You were nothing before you married me. Go back to that stupid family of yours and rot. You'll be sorry when I'm out in California and making loads of money. I can find somebody who will really love me and always put me first."

If the narcissist still needs you, he won't want you upsetting his plans. Your leaving gives you more emotional strength and power in the relationship by moving you further out of the narcissist's control, and he doesn't want that to happen.

Guilt

Guilt is a powerful tool for the narcissist to use to pull you back into the relationship. The narcissist brings up every time he has done something nice for you, or stresses how much he cares about you, or reminds you of the wonderful times you've had together. If the positives don't work to bring you back, narcissists default to their devaluing attacks. Any complaint you have made about the narcissist will be returned and blamed on you. Narcissists consistently blame their partners for behaviors they are actually doing in that very moment, such as screaming, name-calling, hostility, selfishness, hatred, and passive-aggressiveness.

Being told you are selfish, unkind, cruel, greedy, stingy, or hurting someone's feelings can be especially painful to a caretaker. You work so hard to never do those behaviors and almost never even have those kinds of feelings, so you feel so wronged. These comments are such a clear indication that the narcissist doesn't know you or see you for who you are, and that can be heartbreaking.

These kinds of accusations also increase your feelings of guilt, so you're more likely to redouble your efforts to prove to the narcissist that you're not that kind of person. That's just what the narcissist wants because it reengages you in the relationship. Once the narcissist has you back interacting, he can keep you feeling powerless, guilty, and participating in the relationship until he's ready to end it.

Demands for Attention

It is easier to leave a narcissist if you cut off as much contact as possible. However, narcissists can be extremely persistent in grabbing your attention. Clients have reported many types of attention-getting behaviors from narcissists who feel rejected, for example: drunk calling in the middle of the night, "accidentally" breaking into your house to get their belongings, hundreds of texts or e-mail messages in a day, constant pleas for you to "explain" why you want to leave—all of which lead to the narcissist's denouncing you for being so negative.

If you have children together, these pleas for attention can go on and on. One client was so anxious from all of this pressure that she actually lost her voice when she saw her former husband. He was so determined to get her attention that he even pressured the court to "order" her to speak to him in public "for the sake of the children." Actually, of course, it was for the sake of his own egotistical need to be acknowledged.

Promises to Change

If persuasion, guilt, and attention-getting behaviors don't pull you back into the relationship, the narcissist pulls out the "promise" to change. Suddenly the narcissist says he understands why you are upset and ready to leave. He appears to be taking responsibility for his behaviors. He promises to go to therapy, do everything you ask, do things your way. He is so, so sorry to have hurt you.

This is a tempting appeal for a caretaker who truly wants the relationship to work. Now it seems that the narcissist finally understands what you've been saying and is ready to make things right. He seems genuinely sincere. You breathe a sigh of relief and hope builds in you again.

Inevitably this hope disintegrates. Narcissists can't stop trying to control you, and they can't seem to control their own behaviors for any length of time. For a while, you think things are getting better. However, when the narcissist gets comfortable in the relationship again, he'll go back to being self-absorbed, inconsiderate, arrogant, insensitive, and blaming. And, of course, if things don't go his way, he's instantly back to the same defensive and antagonistic patterns. How many times you are willing to believe the narcissist's false promises is up to you.

Social Attacks and Gossip

It is hard to keep the end of your relationship with a narcissist out of the public eye, because the narcissist demands that everyone you know choose sides. As soon as possible he will tell your friends, neighbors, church members, and club acquaintances in person and on social media *his* version of the story of your breakup. That is very distressful for most caretakers. During your entire relationship, the narcissist insisted on extreme privacy about your interactions together, and now he is spreading all kinds of misinformation and slander and trying to ruin your good name. Too often caretakers continue to keep their promises not to talk about the relationship, which ends up letting the narcissist's lies stand without response.

Gossip is a manipulative tactic designed to make you the bad guy and the narcissist to gain as much sympathy as possible. It can also work effectively to reengage you with him and bring you under control.

Stalking

Although stalking is usually not blatant or threatening by narcissists, it is not uncommon for narcissists to fortuitously be at the grocery store when you are there, suddenly appear at a community or social event you attend, or change their running schedule to go down your street every morning. Be prepared ahead of time for these unexpected meetings. They're designed to keep you aware of the narcissist's presence and emotionally off balance.

Neediness

Narcissists appear to be strong and independent, but they are actually extremely needy. You may find it hard to let go of taking care of the narcissist. You may get calls to come fix her car, or he may still expect you to keep doing the accounting for his business, or she wants you to take down the Christmas lights on her house, or he expects you to still make his dentist appointments. It can be exhausting and difficult for you to say no to these persistent requests. Too often you get pulled back into interactions with the narcissist that really don't benefit you.

CONCLUSION

Narcissists try to be in control of all aspects of their relationships. They want to decide when and how to leave, and they want to make sure that you and everyone else believes it is your fault. The reasons that narcissists decide to leave a relationship have little or nothing to do with you. It is likely that even the narcissist doesn't know the real reasons. However, when a narcissist has decided to leave, there is very little a partner can do to stop it from happening.

When you try to leave, you face a barrage of persuasion tactics that can be overwhelming and intimidating because the narcissist tries to make you feel guilty and completely to blame.

The narcissist seems only to care about how others see him, with little or no concern for anyone else's feelings. It's his goal to look as good as possible and maintain control.

QUESTIONS FOR REFLECTION

What blame have you taken on for the end of this relationship?

What do you think are the *real* reasons the narcissist left this relationship?

How have you been trying to fix, repair, or save this relationship? What has been the result?

How has the narcissist been trying to make you the "bad guy"?

How did the narcissist in your life leave?

Have you ever thought about or tried to leave the narcissist? What happened?

How does the narcissist try to pull you back in to interactions with him or her?

5

WHAT JUST HAPPENED?

"If you're going through hell, keep going."
—Winston Churchill

When you found out that the narcissist was leaving, you began a process of adjusting to that information. It may help to know the feelings that most caretakers experience in the course of being rejected by a narcissist so that you can see that what you are experiencing is normal.

Shock—This Is Not the Same Person

At the beginning of the relationship the narcissist was charming, warm, affectionate, often witty, and confident. Yes, you probably also saw his arrogance, self-absorption, and moodiness, but those things seemed fleeting or you thought they were something you could help him overcome. The narcissist had probably been through a number of relationships, which he probably described as awful, horrible, or crazy. You thought that your love, loyalty, kindness, and sympathy would guarantee that the narcissist would never think of you in those terms. But in spite of all you have given, here you are being rejected and rebuffed anyway. In addition, you may now feel that somehow this is all your fault.

It comes as a huge shock when the narcissist turns from Dr. Jekyll into Mr. Hyde. The moment the narcissist first switched is significant for most caretakers. It may even have felt like an actual electrical shock going through your body. Many people see the first glimpse of that change occurring at a major life turning point, such as the day of your engagement, immediately after the wedding, the birth of your first child, when you signed the papers on an expensive house, when you first caught him in a lie, or some other stress point in your lives together. You brushed it off and tried to repress the feeling, but it rose up again and again at intervals.

As time went by, the narcissist responded more and more with anger, hostility, put-downs, defensiveness, and blame. You worked hard to be forgiving, accepting, flexible, and accommodating. You started protecting your awareness from this negativity by "forgetting" or repressing the memories of these hurtful and injurious behaviors. So even though you had seen the narcissist's mean side many times, you put it out of your mind, ignored it, or told yourself he was just under stress, tired, or depressed. You made excuses, ignored the behavior, and mostly remembered it only when it was aimed at other people—his former wife, his boss, a clerk, or an inattentive waitress. You didn't like that behavior, but you felt it was your job to forgive, forget, and move forward.

But the narcissist's dark side doesn't go away or magically transform. It's a part of his core personality. The closer you come emotionally to the narcissist, the more you see it. You may have been stunned and surprised by this breakup, but subconsciously you had also been on guard and wary of that hidden part of your loved one for a long time.

Confusion—What's Going to Happen Now?

Relationships with narcissists are continually confusing because they have two strongly opposing sides to their personalities—the charming, attractive, and positive False Self and the negative, childish, and selfish hidden self. After you were committed and the narcissist relaxed into being himself, both of these selves started appearing side by side, switching from moment to moment. Since then everything has become crazy and confusing. The two parts of the narcissist say entirely different things, want different solutions, and respond to what you say and do in very dissimilar ways.

You may feel that it's impossible for you to figure out what is going to happen next. The "nice part" of the narcissist gives you hope of reconciliation, agrees to go to therapy, sounds concerned, and offers hope that he will change. The angry, mean persona is curt, says hurtful things, and is dismissive and uncaring. So how do you figure out whether you are going to stay or leave? Will you fight to keep the relationship or walk away and give up? Every time you take a step to reconcile, the narcissist pushes you away; however, when you cut off communication or don't answer his e-mails and texts, he demands that you respond and stay engaged. Just when you start to feel more at ease without the narcissist around, he makes overtures to reunite or resume the relationship. It's completely crazy making.

Denial—It Must Be Something I Did

If you are in the early stages of the separation process, you may still want to keep the relationship. You want to remain hopeful. You may believe that you can still do something to save this relationship. One way to put off "the end" is to think that you have the power to change things. It feels comforting to think that you can fix things by saying something different or giving in more. Much of the advice from family, friends, and even professionals encourages you to try harder, improve your communication, be more sympathetic, compromise, be more loving, open up more, give in, and not be so selfish.

I want to emphasize that as a caretaker, you've already done too much of those things. You've probably kept this relationship going much longer than the narcissist has ever experienced before. In fact, that may be part of the problem for the narcissist. He has reached the limit of his ability to tolerate this closeness, far exceeding his comfort zone. You now see the narcissist's faults and shortcomings, and he knows you want him to change. Unfortunately, the narcissist likes being a narcissist and doesn't want to change. He wants out of the relationship but also wants you and everyone else to give him permission to leave and still be the "good guy."

Remember, it's not about you, and it's not your fault. You cannot fix it. Your denial of these truths will lead to more and more pain, confusion, and heartbreak. You don't have the power to change a narcissist. And even if you think you have saved things up to this point, it's extremely unlikely the relationship will be preserved in the long run.

Holding On—I Won't Give Up

When the narcissist is determined to leave the relationship, no amount of holding on will stop him. You can make demands, try reasoning, plead, beg, cry, or get socially kindhearted professionals on your side— minister, therapist, lawyer—but the narcissist will still leave if he wants to. Nothing will save a relationship when one person refuses to participate.

It is likely that the narcissist has broken every promise he has ever made to you. Ask yourself these questions: Do you feel loved, honored, respected, and cared for? Does the narcissist share his intimate feelings with you? Has the narcissist been loyal? Does he kindly and generously share possessions or money with you? Does the narcissist share the responsibilities of maintaining the relationship, the home, the children? Does he nurture and support your emotional well-being and growth? Do you feel safe and comfortable and relaxed in his presence? If these things are missing most of the time, you might wonder what you are holding on to.

Anger—How Could He Do This to Me?

When you start feeling anger, it's a good sign that you are accepting the truth of what is going on. Probably you should have gotten angry a long time ago, but your repression and denial kept your anger in check. When you face the reality that the narcissist is emotionally disabled, unwilling to change, and doesn't understand or care very much about your feelings, that *should* trigger your anger—anger at the narcissist, anger at yourself, maybe even anger at God.

The narcissist has rarely appreciated what you have given in this relationship, and you have given much, much more empathy, time, energy, and attention to him than you have received. That has been unfair. Your faith that things would eventually reach a balance has not proven true. In fact, in this breakup process, the narcissist is still going to believe that you didn't give enough.

Hold on to this anger, but don't expect it to be your only sustaining emotion. Some amount of anger will help you stand up for your rights. Use your anger to motivate you to protect and take care of yourself in this breakup process. However, beware of ongoing, unremitting anger, which can lead to spitefulness, vindictiveness, and petty obsessions about specific hurts and grievances. Chronic anger eventually leads you to a deep loss of self-esteem and increasing victimhood.

Hurt—Pain, Agony, and Relief

You had great hopes and dreams about how this relationship would be—many built on the promises from the narcissist. The hurt and pain you are feeling now come from losing the good feelings and positive elements you actually had in this relationship, but even *more* from the loss of the dream that you had with the narcissist. A big part of any relationship with a narcissist is the fantasy and vision that you thought you shared. Unfortunately, it was just an illusion, a myth, a mirage created by the narcissist. Yes, he totally believed in it as did you, but the fallacy is that the narcissist just can't deliver on those promises. He can't truly be your soul mate because of his inability to be empathetic, emotionally vulnerable, and deeply committed. When the narcissist can't deliver, he just comes up with a new dream that he expects you to automatically accept. When you feel hurt, angry, or blindsided by these sudden changes in the narcissist, you are accused of being negative or obstructionist. That loss can be painful and baffling.

Being abandoned, wrongly accused, demeaned, and criticized is distressing and can shatter your sense of who you are and where your life is going. Combined with the confusing push/pull messages from the narcissist, you can feel adrift, with no anchor or stability. It can lead you to doubt everything that you thought was true.

Seeing your life now as yours alone can be stressful and disturbing. However, if you're starting to see that you have a pattern of getting into caretaking relationships, now is a good time to reassess your views, beliefs, and assumptions about relationships that may have led you into this relationship with a narcissist. Do you honestly want to keep taking care of someone else? Wouldn't you like to be in a relationship that truly meets your needs as well? Do you need to learn skills to stand up for yourself? Will you ever be able to get someone to take what you feel and want seriously?

Even though you miss the narcissist and have a lot of pain and hurt, there is likely a part of you that also feels some sense of relief. Years ago, I gave a narcissistic husband and a caretaking wife the homework assignment to not talk or interact with each other until they came back for their session the next week. When I saw them again, the husband berated me for the horrible and stupid assignment, but the wife said it was the best two days of peace she had had in years. He wasn't able to keep quiet for even an hour, but she had kept at it for two days, ignoring him, cooking only for herself, talking with her friends, and going about her day as she chose. He couldn't stand it. It gave her the insight she needed to realize how much of her time and energy he was using up every day for his emotional needs. Pay attention to those feelings of quiet, calm, and reprieve. How does it feel not to have to constantly pay attention, respond, listen, and deal with the narcissist's ongoing, never-ending neediness and drama?

Revenge, Self-Condemnation, Depression, and Fear

These are what I call the dead-end feelings. They are likely to surface as you make your way through this challenging and confusing time. These are the feelings that will make everything you're going through harder and lengthier.

Seeking revenge may temporarily take your attention off of a skewed belief that the narcissist is somehow "winning," but it only truly feels satisfying to people who are vindictive and bitter. By the end of this book, I hope you can see that the narcissist never wins. He may get things he wants or shape situations to his liking, but he will never feel deep, abiding love and satisfaction. He will never have that relaxed, comfortable feeling of being safely cherished and valued without judgment by another. He will always be stuck in his own fears, vulnerabilities, and defensiveness.

Narcissists would like their partners to dissolve into self-condemnation and helpless shame. It helps them feel less guilty and supports their belief that it is not their fault. However, self-blame, shame, and self-criticism are highly detrimental to making the changes and adaptions you need to do right now. Self-judgments and disapproval drain your energy and demolish your courage. However, self-awareness *without* reproachful judgments can bring deep transformation in your ability to love yourself and be encouraging and responsive to others. I will be showing you ways to make these kinds of changes in later chapters.

Your life has been shaken to the core. Your giving in to the narcissist and taking care of everything you thought he needed, even your giving up your own needs and wants, did not save the relationship. Continuing now to take care of the narcissist while this relationship is ending can lead to your being emotionally and financially harmed even more. Now is the time to back away, catch your breath, and think through what *you* want to do next.

It's important that you do not collapse into depression and fear. You may have periods of feeling hopeless and helpless; however, now is the time to learn new coping strategies and bring your focus to your own self-care. It is a good time to turn your amazing caretaking skills toward your own well-being.

QUESTIONS FOR REFLECTION

When was the first time you saw the dark side of the narcissist? How did you feel in that moment? What did you think? What did you do?

What is currently confusing you about the conflicting behaviors and responses you see from the narcissist?

How have you denied and downplayed the narcissist's negative behaviors?

How do you buy into the narcissist's accusations and complaints about you? Which ones do you believe?

How do you keep hanging on to the narcissist as she or he tries to depart?

Identify and write out a statement about your anger at the narcissist. Keep it handy for when he or she tries to pull you back in.

How are you secretly relieved to be away from the narcissist?

What is your secret revenge scenario?

What triggers you to feel collapsed and hopeless?

6

COPING WITH THE END

"Fall down seven times, rise eight times, life begins now."
—Japanese proverb

Making it through the demise of a relationship with a narcissist can be a harrowing experience. Everything that you believed in and expected from the narcissist gets completely turned upside down. In the beginning of the relationship you were on a pedestal. Now that things don't please the narcissist, you're pushed off and deposed, open to insult, slander, and denigration. You see the dark side of the narcissist in ways you may only have glimpsed before.

NARCISSISTIC RAGE

It doesn't matter whether the narcissist is divorcing you or you are divorcing the narcissist; he will be angry, hostile, and even enraged because his fantasy—delusion—of how things were supposed to be hasn't worked out and it's all your fault. You didn't follow the script; you didn't play your part properly; you said or did the wrong thing. You are the cause, which makes you disloyal, untrustworthy, treacherous, and dishonest.

Source of the Rage

Why is the narcissist so angry at you? Heinz Kohut[1] coined the term "narcissistic rage." He explains that it occurs because the narcissist feels "shame at being faced with failure." This shame, which is hidden deeply within the narcissist, is one of the worst feelings that narcissists experience. As a result, they feel afraid, out of control, and victimized, which they abhor. Kohut says they have a "need for revenge, for righting a wrong, for undoing a hurt by whatever means"[2] They need to be the persecutor to keep from feeling like the victim. Their rage is the result of abject fear that others will see them as imperfect, as losers, and as defective. The narcissist's whole sense of self-esteem is built on being perfect, but the end of a relationship announces to the world that the narcissist is a failure.

Beware of Rescuing

As the narcissist wavers between being the victim and the persecutor, it may seem that the only thing for you to do is try to be a rescuer. Taking any one of these three typical roles—rescuer, victim, or persecutor—keeps you under the control of the narcissist and gives you no powerful way to protect yourself or disengage.

You have spent a great deal of time in the role of rescuer with the narcissist, trying to smooth things over and keep the narcissist calm and comfortable. When you were on the pedestal, you could use your comforting and pacifying skills to good advantage. The narcissist was willing to listen to you and calm down. Now that the narcissist sees you as the enemy, those same behaviors may be interpreted by the narcissist as you trying to control and take advantage of him. Continuing to be a rescuer, placater, and peacemaker is definitely against your best interests.

Your rescuing efforts also signal to the narcissist that you are still willing to give in to his wants. It will not improve your interactions with the narcissist to allow him back into the house, adjust child visitation times and days, ignore late alimony or child maintenance payments, or even have sex or go on vacation together after you have separated. When you are not absolutely clear about your limits and boundaries, you'll have little or no leverage with the narcissist to bring about the conclusions you want.

Narcissists use rage to get what they want and also to keep from emotionally collapsing. Narcissists keep increasing their anger until they feel safe again—which is likely to be quite a while after the divorce is final.[3]

Camille found it hard to come to the conclusion that her marriage was over. She realized that Sydney was a narcissist, but her strong religious convictions kept her trying to help him get over his rages. She tolerated his hurtful name-calling and put-downs. Finally, in another argument over money he grabbed her hand and wrenched it backward, breaking her thumb. In the emergency room, the doctor told her that he was obliged to report the incident as domestic abuse, and it finally became clear to Camille that she, in fact, had been emotionally and psychologically abused for years as well.

WHAT TO EXPECT

No Mutual Parting

A frequent hope and goal for most caretakers is to have a mutual and friendly parting from the narcissist. It's becoming a cultural value and sign of a "successful" divorce to remain friends, use mediation instead of an adversarial approach, coparent, and continue a semifamilial relationship with your former spouse for the benefit of the children. As a therapist, I am completely in favor of all of these goals. However, few divorces involving a narcissist can make these approaches work.

When narcissists are in a rage, they want payback, revenge, and to win. It becomes the narcissist against you. They feel threatened to the core, and the only way for them to feel safe again is to win, and that means to them that you have to lose. Narcissists may identify winning by how much money and property they get, how often their choices and preferences win over yours, or how successful they are in stealing your friends or getting your kids to like them better. Narcissists *want* a competition no matter what they say. There is almost no mutual, amicable, friendly parting. If you allow yourself to get into this competition, you'll experience plenty of pain, grief, and anguish.

It's All Mine

For the majority of narcissists, money is the only sure thing they trust, so they want as much of it as they can get. Male narcissists who made more money than their female partners frequently think that all the money belongs to them in the first place. Many of them have talked their wives out of working, but during a divorce, blame them for not "contributing." They expect to keep all of the assets. In some cases, all of the assets may already be in the narcissist's name alone, so it can be difficult to get your reasonable share.

When your relationship appears to be ending, tread cautiously and have a plan. For you to leave this relationship safely, you'll need a lot of assistance, including a lawyer who has extensive experience with narcissists. Karyl McBride's book *Will I Ever Be Free of You?* offers excellent guidance about the legal process of getting out of a relationship with a narcissist.[4] Having control of your assets, a place to live, and a way to support yourself ahead of time will help a lot. You'll also need a strong emotional support system to sustain you, including friends, family members, a knowledgeable therapist, and spiritual support.

Get your own lawyer as soon as possible. If you haven't seen this coming, you may also need to get a forensic accountant busy to find all of your joint assets before the narcissist hides them or empties the accounts. If you have been handling the finances, you may know where the money and assets are. If the narcissist handled the money, it may be hard to find it and get what is financially fair for you.

As soon as the narcissist acknowledges there will be a divorce, he typically starts talking about cooperation, working together, and coming to settlement agreement without lawyers, citing the expense and hostility that lawyers bring to the situation. But this is usually a ruse to divide property and assets to his advantage by dominating, pressuring, and intimidating you into giving him what he wants.

You definitely need your own lawyer. You need someone on your side, with your interests in mind, who will speak up for your rights. Even trained professionals can find it intimidating to stand up to the narcissist's rage and manipulation, so as a caretaker who has loved this person, you have little chance of defending yourself adequately. In their rage, narcissists may threaten to leave you penniless, homeless, and bankrupt, and many of them do try. Get familiar with the laws in your state, and hire a lawyer who knows what he or she is doing.

What About the Kids?

Narcissists parent in many different ways. However, they tend to go to extremes—either being overly attentive or disregarding. The narcissist who previously ignored and didn't participate much in parenting may suddenly become a "superparent," especially doing lots of fun things so the kids will still like him. He may use the children as companions so he won't be alone. He may put more intense pressure on the children to perform well to prove the divorce isn't hurting them. Or he may decide to become their teacher, coach, or trainer for activities that are of particular interest to him. Trying to establish a coparenting plan that works for the children and for you can be difficult, because the narcissist's needs are always more important.

Sometimes narcissists become overly focused on their children in a divorce, and use them to expand their conflict with you so as to increase your feelings of being devalued, frightened, or a failure. These kinds of self-enhancing behaviors can ebb and flow throughout your children's childhood. Again, be careful not to get pulled into being a rescuer, persecutor, or victim. That will only prolong the conflict, which can have negative effects on your children.

Fifty/fifty child custody is especially desired by narcissists—even if they have done little or no child care previously—because it eliminates the requirement for paying child support in most states. It's not uncommon, however, for the narcissist to gain fifty/fifty custody only to, within months or years, turn most of the parenting over to you again or to a new spouse while still paying no child support. Narcissists typically become less and less interested in interacting with their children when the children develop their own interests, individuality, and opinions. The children's increasing independence can bring up the same behaviors from the narcissist of idealizing and then devaluing them that happened to you in the marriage, and can create a lot of conflict.

On the other hand, I've been amazed at how well kids can see and handle the narcissist's emotional disabilities when they have you as a role model of strength. When you refuse to take the narcissist's comments personally and you set limits and boundaries and speak up for yourself, your children will learn how to handle themselves with the narcissist more effectively.

Of course, this does not cover all that you need and want to know about how your kids will be affected by having a narcissistic parent. There are many good books about this, so take time to read them and share with your children when you feel they are old enough.

HOW TO RESPOND

Staying out of the drama triangle of victim, persecutor, and rescuer is essential to navigating this experience. The longer you have been involved with a narcissist and immersed in this drama pattern, the harder it can be. You may feel very victimized, or your anger and resentment may trigger a strong need to persecute the narcissist, or you may automatically go into caretaker mode without even being aware of doing it. Keep checking on yourself to keep from falling into any of these three roles. Throughout the rest of this book you'll find many strategies to keep yourself centered and out of these old roles. When you feel strong and prepared to deal with the narcissist in new ways, you'll be better able to protect yourself and maintain your equilibrium.

Defuse Your Fear

You immediately need to work on lowering your levels of fear and anxiety. Narcissistic rage is something awful to behold and can be terribly frightening to have aimed directly at you. The narcissist wants you to feel threatened and anxious so you can't think. Then you'll more easily give in to what he wants. Narcissists believe that you deserve to feel bad for causing them to feel and look like a failure. A humiliated narcissist can be quite menacing and intimidating.

Don't believe the narcissist's dire and threatening predictions about your future, but also don't ignore his threats. Take steps immediately to protect yourself both physically and psychologically. Taking action can help defuse your fear. Change the locks on the doors, open a separate bank account, close or remove your name from all the joint credit cards, and stop making any requests for help from the narcissist. Don't respond to hostile e-mails or texts, and keep copies of all verbal and written threats in a special notebook. It would be ideal if you did these things during the first days after separation. However, it's been my experience that most caretakers don't even think to do these things for weeks or months. The sooner you do them, the sooner you'll start feeling more in control.

If you find yourself shaking, unable to think, unable to eat, startling easily, and inundated with anxiety, you will need to calm these feelings before you can do much of anything. This is the time to remember to breathe. That may sound simplistic, but it is essential that you consciously pay attention to your breathing. People in fear have a tendency to stop breathing or to hyperventilate. Both of these reactions interfere with oxygen getting to your brain, heart, and other primary organs. Not breathing will also trigger your freeze response. When your brain and body freeze and shut down, you can't think, remember things, or make rational decisions. At those times, you may find yourself more willing to give in to the narcissist's demands, give up your rights, or even beg the narcissist to come back just to ease your panic and fear. So breathing is essential for your mental health and your physical needs.

Task

Sit or lie down somewhere comfortable and quiet. Put one hand over your heart and one hand on your diaphragm. Slowly breathe in, feeling your lower hand and then your upper hand move out as your lungs fill with air. Then slowly breathe out, feeling your lungs deflate and your shoulders drop. Do this to the count of four—four counts on the in breath and four counts on the out breath. Most people find that doing this breathing series even four or five times starts the relaxation process. If you are in deep distress, you may need to do this for ten to twenty minutes.

This exercise is *not* a waste of time. Your body may be so tense that you can't fully relax, but it will help clear your mind enough to think again. It brings your cognitive functions back on line. If you find that your body stays so tense that you find it painful to breathe and you can't sleep, then a relaxation or sleep medication may be helpful for a while. Used carefully, these medications can help you keep your panic in check. Talk with your doctor about what you are going through and ask what is right for you.

Find Support

No one can deal alone with the kind of situation you are going through. You need someone to listen so you can decompress, empty out your teeming thoughts, and get back on track. You also need validation that you're not crazy and assurance that you can handle this. A therapist with extensive knowledge about the narcissist and caretaker patterns and a nonjudgmental, non-advice-giving best friend are a minimal support team. Reading books, joining a support group, and staying active with at least some weekly social activities also help. Although you may find it hard to ask for help, remember that this is a serious situation, and you need to reach out for support. It is necessary for both your emotional and physical health.

Disengage

The best way to protect yourself from a hostile narcissist is to disengage. Yes, the narcissist hates that, but he 's already in a rage anyway and it is no longer your job to take care of his feelings. Now is the time to think about your own emotional needs. Lawyers consistently tell their clients to quit responding and interacting with the narcissist and do all communicating through them until the divorce is over, but they say their clients rarely listen to them. I want to reinforce this recommendation. Until a final settlement is reached, narcissists will try every means possible to keep you emotionally distraught and off balance with what they say and do.

Disengagement is more than not talking, texting, e-mailing, or interacting. It also includes *emotionally* letting go (more about this in the next chapter). To emancipate yourself from the narcissist, you have to quit caring what he thinks of you. You also need to let go of any dependence on the narcissist—emotional, physical, and financial. If you have young children, it may take years to completely disengage. But you can begin to separate yourself emotionally when you quit allowing the narcissist to be your judge, the person who defines you, the person whose opinion is most important to you, and the person who controls your emotions.

Disengagement means taking back control of your life instead of letting the narcissist determine your feelings. Get the narcissist out of your head as your judge and jury *right now*, and you'll find you feel significantly better, more optimistic, more creative, and happier.

Be Businesslike

As you become more disengaged from the narcissist, you can start treating your interactions with him in a more businesslike manner. In business, emotional responses are relegated to the background, and people try to talk about only the specific issue at hand. At work you try your best to be cordial, even when you don't like somebody. You may disagree, but there is no name-calling, rude remarks, or hostile body language. You don't cry, beg, or share your intimate feelings with your work associates. Your interactions will go better with the narcissist if you follow this same model.

The narcissist used to be your closest and most trusted companion—the person whose responses mattered more to you than anyone else's. That is gone. He now sees you as the enemy. So when you continue to expect that the narcissist will consider your feelings or entreaties, you'll probably be deeply disappointed, and your requests will trigger his guilt and hostility.

Being businesslike gives you more power. Be calm and rational, stick close to the topic, and refuse to be sidetracked. When you stay calm, the narcissist is the only one reacting emotionally and looks more clearly like the crazy person he is. Don't be intimidated or embarrassed by the narcissist's horrible behavior. It's all right for information about the narcissist's genuinely dreadful side to be visible to others. This makes the truth about his behaviors clear. You used to enable the narcissist by keeping those behaviors hidden, but it will do you no good now. It may be a tremendous relief to you to quit covering up, and it allows the rest of the world to see the narcissist more authentically. I'm not suggesting that you gossip or talk derogatorily about the narcissist. Simply state true facts without covering them up. Stop apologizing for the narcissist, and quit dismissing or explaining his rude and negative behaviors. You do not want to bad-mouth the narcissist to friends, family, or your children. Speak only the truth about the actual behaviors and words of the narcissist. Overall it is best to let people see for themselves how the narcissist acts under stress, which just requires you to stop covering it all up.

Take Excellent Care of Yourself

When you focus on putting exercise, healthy food, and good self-care into your daily schedule, you'll find yourself feeling more powerful and doing less worrying. Actively taking care of your body automatically improves your self-esteem and prepares you to handle challenges. Moving your body helps balance your breathing, brings oxygen to your brain, and gets your heart pumping. These actions help keep you from shutting down emotionally or dropping into depression. Get a massage, sit in a hot tub, or do whatever helps you to relax. Make your own physical well-being a priority.

I also recommend that you keep a journal of your thoughts and feelings. It's surprisingly calming and validating to put down on paper your experiences and insights. It can help you sort through the confusion and figure out what you want to do about this huge change. It's also a good memory trigger to help you stop "forgetting" and diminishing those negative interactions with the narcissist.

Now is not the time to be stingy with yourself. Invest in your health and healing. Put your time and money into services that provide good emotional care. Taking care of yourself is not selfish; it is good sense. It will also pay off for your friends, children, and loved ones in less worry and distress for them too.

QUESTIONS FOR REFLECTION

What elements of narcissistic rage have you seen from your partner?

How are you still trying to rescue or appease the narcissist?

What hopes are you still hanging onto that this relationship will be saved?

How likely is it that you'll get cooperation from the narcissist in your situation?

What are your concerns for your children in this split?

What actions are you taking to reduce your fears?

How disengaged are you from the narcissist at the present time? What could you do to disengage further?

What new, more businesslike behaviors could you put into practice?

What have you been covering up for the narcissist? How can you quit covering these things up?

How well are you taking care of yourself? What else could you do?

7

LETTING GO

"Don't look backwards; you aren't going that way."
—Autumn Shields, author of *Living Your Life Alive*

Relationships with narcissists frequently end no matter how hard you try to save them.

The end is often painful, exhausting, and generally upsetting. Whether your relationship ends, hangs together for months or years, or settles into a rhythm that you can live with, you will need to learn to let go of many of the expectations, hopes, and dreams you have had about how you wanted it to work. Changing your perspective, presumptions, reactions, and strategies will reduce your frustration, emotional injuries, and general distress.

CHANGE YOUR PERSPECTIVE

By now you understand that the narcissist's views of the world, relationships, and of you are distorted, and his reactions aren't normal. The most common reason you continually get blindsided by the narcissist's reactions is that you keep thinking that he'll react normally. It's especially difficult to keep this in mind when the narcissist seems to be talking and interacting more conventionally for a period of time. You get to thinking that he is back to center and will now be reasonable. But the narcissist's twisted views will always resurface, so you need to be prepared.

Narcissists Will Always Be Narcissistic

Perhaps one of the hardest things to come to terms with is accepting that the person you loved is mentally ill. I actually prefer to use the term "emotionally disabled," because it more accurately describes the situation. These emotional disabilities are always there, although the narcissist can sometimes override them. When his False Self is in place, he can appear quite normal, relaxed, funny, entertaining, and charming. But don't be fooled into thinking that everything is all right. He will inevitably reverse again. Always keep in mind that the narcissist is emotionally impaired, and be prepared for him to "malfunction."

Overcome Your Fear of Being Judgmental

Most caretakers trip themselves up, because they find it hard to make any negative judgments about other people. Identifying narcissistic traits in another person is not much different from recognizing that someone has blue eyes, is tall or short, or is right or left handed. Distinguishing personality traits in yourself and others can be tremendously helpful for predicting what behaviors and actions will occur in particular situations. If you're willing to acknowledge only positive characteristics, then you'll be woefully unprepared to deal with the narcissist's negative actions.

Take away the positive and negative labels and try to see the narcissist's traits as simply an informational list of behaviors. It is also helpful to acknowledge that all of us have traits that we like or dislike, that are functional in certain situations and not in others, or that are helpful or detrimental to ourselves or others. For instance, a highly active person who takes charge and is innovative and creative would be great in suddenly dangerous and unknown situations but would probably not make a good grocery store clerk. The narcissist's personality characteristics work effectively to protect his immature and fragile ego. These same behaviors, however, can be very harmful to you and others. Not taking the *entire spectrum* of the narcissist's behaviors into consideration each and every time you interact could be foolish and hazardous. Don't ignore some behaviors or traits just because you don't want to be judgmental or negative.

Quit Caretaking

A major part of being a caretaker in this relationship has been the requirement to be the nice one, to give in, make things right, deal with any problems and difficulties, and spare the narcissist any anxiety or upset. That role has to face a major overhaul if you're going to regain your independence and emotional well-being. You have to stop taking care of the narcissist and start focusing on caring for yourself. That may be a challenge, and you may find you don't have many ideas about how to do that.

The first step is to quit thinking about the narcissist all the time. Instead, pay attention to what *you* are feeling and what *you* are wanting to do. Each time you start wondering what the narcissist thinks or feels about this or that, turn your attention back to yourself. This takes concentration and practice at first, but with repetition, it'll become easier and feel more natural. When you put more energy and focus on your own life and needs, you'll come up with more creative and effective ways to care for yourself, and you'll start healing.

It is no longer your job to take care of the narcissist. Caretakers often say to me that they need to keep focusing on the narcissist as a way to protect themselves from what the narcissist might do next. If you clearly identify and remember the narcissist's behaviors, you'll be prepared enough. It's when you forget that the narcissist will act like a narcissist that you find yourself in trouble. When you disengage from caretaking and put more energy into observing and accepting the narcissist *as he is*, you'll be much better protected and less surprised.

Focus on You

Most caretakers keep obsessing about the narcissist, because it has become a habit. Like all habits, you need to catch yourself when you're caretaking, stop yourself in that moment, and have a new behavior ready to take its place. That's a good time to tune in to your own feelings, and consider what *you* want to do. Right now you may think you feel numb or you don't have a clue what you are feeling. Here's a way to tune in to your own feelings more.

Task

Draw a circle on a piece of paper, and then cut it into four wedges. In each wedge, write a feeling you are having right this minute. If you get stuck with only three feelings, repeat the one that is the strongest. Don't be surprised if all the feelings don't seem to go together, for example, angry, frustrated, hurt, and relieved. Think about each feeling until you discover what event brought that feeling to the surface (e.g., I was hurt when Jim cut me off in midsentence). Then try to pinpoint the self-judgment, conclusion, or assumption that triggered the feeling (e.g., I felt discounted and unimportant). Finally, decide what you want to do about that feeling (e.g., I know I'm important to my children and friends, and it no longer matters what Jim thinks of me).

This exercise can take anywhere from a few minutes to hours or days to do, depending on how easily you can identify your feelings and what event or thought triggered them. Were you able to identify four feelings? Did you figure out what triggered those feelings in you? How aware of your own thoughts and self-judgments are you? Were you able to figure out what you want to do to change what you are experiencing? You have been trying to figure out the narcissist in this same way. Now is the time to focus on your own feelings.

CHANGE YOUR REACTIONS

The way you have been reacting to the narcissist's behaviors has to be changed so you can move forward with your life. You also need to protect yourself from further emotional damage. It's time to stop being controlled by the narcissist's need to make everything about being superior/inferior, good/bad, right/wrong, or win/lose. Those patterns lead to anger, hurt, fear, and anxiety and ultimately have been at the core of much of your suffering and distress.

Let Go of Winning and Losing

Winning and losing matter only in relation to someone else—in this case, the narcissist. Does he get more money than you think is fair? Does he get more time with the kids than you prefer? Do you now have to work longer hours than you want? Will you have to sell your house and move? You think you win if you get what you want and lose if you don't.

When you let go of trying to control outcomes, you'll feel better in the long run. The narcissist is all about control, getting what he wants, looking better than you, being more successful, or having a better life. You'll always feel like a loser when you compete with a narcissist. Narcissists spend every free moment trying to look good and get what they want. Unless you're willing to put in that same amount of time and energy into those same things, the narcissist will probably "win." So the only way out of that rivalry is to step away and quit trying to compete. You can't lose if you're not in the game.

Getting out of the game can be tricky. The narcissist is very determined to keep you in the game. He can't win if you aren't playing. The narcissist hides money so you get less and then spends it on a fancy new car. He sends e-mails and photos to show you how happy he is in his new relationship. These things are designed to make you feel like a loser. The only way out is to let go of comparing yourself in any way to the narcissist, and stop caring what the narcissist says or does. To accomplish this, you'll have to get away from his influence on your life and create a life that is closer to what you want for yourself.

Only You Have the Right to Judge Yourself

When you're with a narcissist, you get used to his judging, approving or disapproving of what you say, do, feel, and want. Now is the time to mark the narcissist off your list of those whose opinions matter to you. That means you quit worrying, obsessing, or even considering what the narcissist thinks of you. It no longer matters. His opinions are totally based on his own biased and twisted views of the world, anyway. He has nothing to do with the reality of who you are. It's time to trust your own judgment.

Try also not to worry too much about what the narcissist says to others about you. People who know and love you can tell that what the narcissist says is off base. People who don't know you as well but are important—your children's teachers, neighbors, members of groups you belong to, or judges and mediators, for instance—need to get a chance to see who you are. Tell them about yourself, your values, and your activities. Don't spend your time talking about the narcissist. As for strangers, whom you'll never meet anyway, ask yourself why it matters what they think.

Stop Hiding—Tell Others What You're Going Through

Caretakers too often feel ashamed, at fault, and responsible for the end of the relationship with a narcissist. You may want to hide and not tell anyone what is happening, or you may find yourself suddenly spewing out all sorts of horrible anecdotes and confidences to people you hardly know. Neither of these approaches will be beneficial.

Start sharing what is going on in your life with a close friend or family member whom you trust. You may never have told anyone about the odd, cruel, tactless, and insensitive behaviors of the narcissist. You may have hidden this part of your life because you were confused, embarrassed, or humiliated by what was going on. People who love and care about you want to be supportive—and you need that support—but they can't be helpful if you don't let them know what you're feeling and needing.

Think through what you want to say and to whom. You don't want to burden everyone with tales of woe, so it's helpful to have explanations that are well thought out and self-respecting. To your nearest and dearest you can be more open and specific about your experiences and feelings. To more casual friends it's appropriate to share in general terms how you are doing, for example, "I'm having a tough day today" or "I'm feeling anxious today; would you like to go to a movie with me to get my mind off things?" With acquaintances you might say "Randy and I are getting a divorce. It hasn't been working out for a while." Don't feel you have to divulge information you don't want to, but also don't portray the narcissist in glowing terms or yourself negatively. Remember, too, that put-downs, labeling, name-calling, hostility, and resentment toward the narcissist are best saved for a neutral party, such as a therapist, who won't be judgmental of you and won't use it against you when you feel more benevolent.

Lastly, don't use your children as sounding boards for your feelings about your intimate relationship. You'll be talking about their father, mother, or grandparent. That puts children in the middle between people they love and count on for security, identity, and self-esteem.

Be Yourself Instead of What Others Want You to Be

Your most familiar response around the narcissist has been to change yourself to meet his expectations—changing your feelings, choices, opinions, even how you dress, or the food you eat. You may also find that some friends and family want you to respond to the narcissist and your relationship differently than you believe will work for you. Remember, *you* are the one going through this experience, and only you can ultimately decide what is best for you to do. A good way to be yourself is to follow your own inclinations and preferences and make the choices that feel best for your well-being.

CHANGE YOUR STRATEGIES

Stop Showing Your Reactions to the Narcissist

Narcissists love getting a reaction from you. To them it's a test of their power and dominance. They know they're pushing your buttons when you have an emotional response. To let go, you need to stop letting the narcissist see his effect on you. Anger, tears, hurt, shock, retorts, or pretty much any strong response feeds the narcissist's need for your attention. He wants out of the relationship, but he wants you to still be attached and emotionally involved with him.

Adopt neutral body language and facial expressions around the narcissist. This helps you set a boundary between the narcissist and yourself. You're no longer going to join in the narcissist's emotional games and competitions. The more you practice this attitude of neutrality, the stronger you'll feel. It helps *you* to move your emotions to the side. As long as you have these strong reactions to the narcissist, you are still enmeshed and involved, and the narcissist can continue to control you.

Restrict Your Contact with the Narcissist

Restricting your contact with the narcissist as much as possible will help you let go and feel better. If you have legal matters to deal with, let your lawyer tackle that for you. If you have children to exchange, have the other parent pick them up from or deliver them to school. If you have to meet face-to-face, use a neutral location if possible to avoid either of you triggering old feelings. Don't respond to e-mails or texts that aren't businesslike or don't have a real purpose. Ignore messages from the narcissist to talk things over, find closure, or tell him why you don't want to get back together. These are setups to get you reengaged and are often ploys to get around the legal agreements you've already made.

Set Real Boundaries and Limits

Because narcissists don't recognize or honor boundaries, they want exceptions to everything. They agree to one thing, and then they demand the right to change it, accusing you of coercing them into it. When they have problems and issues, they want you to fix them. They scream hateful things at you and then call in the middle of the night and want your sympathy.

Decide what you will and won't put up with and stick to it. When these boundaries are put into legal agreements, honor them exactly— even if sometimes you would also like exceptions. To the narcissist, any exception you make essentially nullifies the whole agreement and signals that he now has the right to make further exceptions. When the narcissist sees that you'll give in on one thing, he'll push for you to give in on more and more.

This is not the time to be nice, flexible, helpful, understanding, or overly considerate. The minute you start feeling sorry for the narcissist, you're back under his spell. Boundaries, limits, and disengagement are all ways to effectively let go. You may also need to set boundaries on yourself as well. For example, don't stalk the narcissist on social media, ask your kids how the other parent is doing, or keep tabs on him in any way. These behaviors will only increase your anxiety, misery, and continued attachment.

Step Away from Conflict

In the past when the narcissist has emotionally attacked, you've probably responded by pushing back or collapsing in hurt. It's time for a new strategy. It's time for emotional aikido. In aikido, the person being attacked watches the attacker carefully to assess where he is going to hit and then calmly twists around or takes a step away so that the blow will miss. This results in the attacker missing or falling. You can learn to do the same.

The steps to this strategy follow: Look the narcissist in the eye. Breathe and stay calm. No matter what he says, respond with "Really? Is that what you think/feel/believe/want? I see." Then walk away. Do not engage, discuss, counterattack, or make any other responses. Simply leave. The narcissist may be astonished, infuriated, continue talking, or whatever. It doesn't matter. You have just taken yourself out of the impending conflict. By refusing to engage unless the interaction is civil, you have changed the rules of the game. Keep it up, and you'll find you have less and less contact with the narcissist and more and more relief.

Protect Yourself

You definitely need to protect yourself from the narcissist's negativity as much as possible. (I'll talk more about this in chapter 13.) The minute the narcissist starts belittling, attacking, or demeaning you, extricate yourself. State the facts of who you are and what you want if necessary and then disengage—walk away or hang up the phone, and don't respond further until everyone cools down.

Don't let the narcissist into your house. Don't drive by his home. Sit with friends and as far away as possible from the narcissist at events you both have to attend. When your mind starts wandering, wondering or worrying about what the narcissist is doing or might do, change your attention and take your mind off of those thoughts. In every way possible, cut the narcissist out of your thoughts and life.

CHANGE YOUR LIFE

Tune In to Yourself

This is a good time to reevaluate your life. You've spent your entire relationship with the narcissist trying to understand him. Now it's time to look inside and figure out who you are. What parts of yourself have you given up to please and accommodate the narcissist? What goals or dreams did you leave behind? What negative thoughts about yourself have you incorporated from his opinions? What things about yourself have you kept hidden and protected? Wake up to who you are, what you enjoy, and the feelings and experiences that bring you joy. Much of the rest of this book will focus on helping you heal these wounds and reconnect with yourself.

Reflect on How You Were Vulnerable to the Narcissist

Have you thought about how and why the narcissist picked you and you picked the narcissist? Ross Rosenberg, in his book *The Human Magnet Syndrome*,[1] identifies characteristics of people who choose continuing, long-term relationships with narcissists, much of which we discussed in chapter 2. As you begin the process of letting go of the narcissist and are better able to look at both of you with less anger and criticism, you'll be more able to reflect on the parts of yourself that may need strengthening and adjusting.

You were chosen by the narcissist and you chose the narcissist for reasons that were probably indiscernible to you at the time. As these traits and tendencies become more visible, let yourself consider what ways you need to grow to fortify yourself against future manipulation by others. Upcoming chapters will help you with this process. The most important element for change, however, is learning to stop judging, criticizing, or invalidating yourself.

Reassess Your Friends

When you end a relationship with a narcissist, you may become aware that you have other narcissistic relationships that you hadn't noticed before. Narcissists can be entertaining and charming, but they make better acquaintances than real friends. Pay attention to who is being supportive of you in this time of loss—those whose comfort feels truly reassuring and soothing versus those who offer advice, dire predictions, or simply launch into their own stories of woe. You don't have to keep a "friend" just because you have known him or her all of your life or you used to like each other years ago. Now is a good time to identify what qualities you find cheering, kind, encouraging, and honest in others and seek out people with the potential to be true, caring friends no matter what is happening. It's OK to let the others go.

Don't Get Stuck in the Past

Looking back to figure out and understand the narcissist's disorder and disabilities can help you anticipate his actions and deal with him more effectively. However, don't get stuck in just analyzing the narcissist. Use what you learn to take better care of yourself. If your thoughts aren't helpful to you in dealing with the present, don't waste your energy on it. Ruminating on the past may be easier than figuring a new life path and learning new skills, but it drains your power in the present.

Future Fears

What fears do you have about your future? Have you lost hope that what you want is possible? Are you letting the narcissist's definition of who you are dominate and overwhelm you? Do you have a core fear about being alone? Do you think you are incapable of handling things on your own? Avoiding your fears only makes them loom larger. Facing your fears helps you start defining them as problems to be confronted and overcome. Fears are nebulous, but seeing them as challenges and dilemmas to be solved makes them more manageable.

Reach Out to New Opportunities

Letting go of the past helps you reach out to new opportunities that are now opening up. The Chinese character for "crisis" is a combination of two words—danger and opportunity. Right now you are probably feeling immersed in the element of danger. After all, a big part of your life, your dreams, as well as your finances, children, and property are all in chaos and turmoil. But every crisis eventually opens up into new prospects, new viewpoints, new people, new possibilities, and new options. You may not have wanted or chosen these new things to come into your life, but they now give you the possibility to benefit, grow, advance, and open up to more of who you are and what you want in your life. You do have choices.

Since you decided to pick up this book and have read this far, I think it is pretty good evidence that you are motivated to move forward. You want to heal. You see there are possibilities in your future that could make your life more of what you want it to be. Let's move forward then to healing, empowering, and transforming this situation into a life where you can thrive and flourish.

QUESTIONS FOR REFLECTION

What changes in your self-image and your view of the narcissist do you need to make?

Which of your reactions to the end of this relationship have been unproductive or futile for you? What reactions would you like to be having instead?

What part of your emotional relationship with the narcissist do you find difficult to let go of?

How ready are you to face down the narcissist and walk away?

What can you do to better protect yourself from the narcissist's attacks and criticisms?

How can you better tune in to yourself and better tune out the narcissist?

How much time do you spend reviewing the past? How can you bring yourself into the present more?

What fears are keeping you from letting go of the narcissist? What else are you hanging onto that is keeping you from moving forward?

III

Healing After the Crash

8

GRIEVING

"Your pain is the breaking of the shell that encloses your understanding."
—Kahlil Gibran, from *The Prophet*

Pain, anger, and grief are all bound up together. Anger keeps the pain of grief and loss at bay until we are strong enough to bear it. Grief expresses our deepest pain so it can come out and be healed. Elizabeth Kubler-Ross says that we go through five stages of grief when we experience a great loss: denial, anger, bargaining, depression, and acceptance.[1] In actuality we circle through these feelings round and round as we heal and slowly come to terms with the truth that our lives are changed forever. Owning and expressing your grief allows you to be aware when you are hurting, angry, and in denial. There is much you can do to heal these feelings as they emerge. It's also helpful to be aware of when you are bargaining with yourself and trying to go back to how things were, which leads you back into the pain. As you lose hope, it can be good to know that your feeling of depression is actually an opening to the possibility of acceptance.

In our very fast, hurry-up-and-get-over-it culture, there is an assumption that grief should last a couple of months and be over. However, it is important to keep in mind that you're mourning many losses when your relationship ends with a narcissist. You've lost a spouse/lover/partner. You've lost the dream of what you believed your life would be like with that person. Your self-esteem has been damaged as a result of the blaming and devaluation by the narcissist. You've probably lost property, money, and financial stability. Your confidence and sense of worth have been shredded. You may have lost half of the time you used to spend with your children. You've lost your relationship goals. And in addition, the narcissist is probably still hanging around threatening to make your life miserable.

DEALING WITH DENIAL

When you've been a caretaker for so long, it's often hard to admit to yourself and others the full extent of the harm you've suffered in your relationship with the narcissist. You're more comfortable paying attention to the narcissist's pain or the effort and promises he is making. You want to keep hoping that if the narcissist just gets help, things will turn around. Exploring your own pain, counting up all that you have lost, and really admitting that you have been abandoned can seem embarrassing and too painful. Your tendency to take all the blame for the failure of the relationship onto yourself may make it harder for you to acknowledge the deep injuries you have sustained.

Acknowledge the Harm That Was Done

You're not to blame for the way the narcissist treated you. Narcissists work hard to keep you off balance and vulnerable. Your goodwill, generosity, and flexibility were taken advantage of. Try looking at the harm that you experienced without judging yourself. It may be difficult for you to stop taking responsibility for how the narcissist treated you, but it's vitally important that you separate his behavior from yours. You did not *make* the narcissist treat you badly. The narcissist chose to treat you that way to avoid feeling bad himself.

Task

Take some time right now to make a list of the harm you believe the narcissist did to you in this relationship. I'm not asking you to dwell on the negative, but it needs to be identified and acknowledged so you can repair those wounds. If you push those things into your subconscious, they can fester and turn to bitterness, fear, anxiety, and self-hatred.

When Anne did this exercise, she was shocked by how long her list was and how many excuses automatically came to mind to "explain" why each one was her fault. Her list included the following: He screamed at me about the dinner—because I burned the potatoes. He was angry and refused to talk to me for two days—because I bought him the wrong tool set for Christmas. He took my car keys away—because I told him I wanted to leave.

Each of these "because" reasons was created to excuse the narcissist's horrible and hurtful behaviors, which were often, in fact, emotional abuse and coercion. Keep in mind that no one should have the right to treat you in these ways. Narcissists act the way they do because they are narcissistic, not because of anything you've done.

Experience the Feelings

When you acknowledge the harm you experienced, it brings up unpleasant and sometimes overwhelming feelings. While you were in the relationship with the narcissist, you felt you needed to avoid these feelings in order to keep going. Instead, you continually focused on the narcissist's feelings and worked to keep things positive, upbeat, and enjoyable for him—and for yourself. During the time that all of those upsetting experiences were happening, it's likely you tried very hard to ignore how hurt you were. That denial of your feelings kept you in the relationship, perhaps longer than was good for you. It also kept you from really seeing, feeling, and being aware of the reality of your abusive situation.

Task

Take some time now to acknowledge your own feelings of hurt, pain, distress, frustration, loss, emotional injury, and whatever else comes up for you. List your feelings as accurately and specifically as possible. In the next chapter we'll use that list for an exercise of healing and repair. For now, just observe and allow those feelings to be present. Honor each one for helping you understand and become more fully aware of what you've been through. This can facilitate your learning to appreciate your strength, loyalty, determination, and stamina. You stayed, you worked hard, and you devoted yourself to trying to heal and repair this relationship as long as you possibly could. You need to respect those

strengths inside yourself and your courage to give so fully and unselfish-
ly to another person.

OPENING TO ANGER

Anger Is Normal

Of course you're angry. Caretakers are more willing to feel hurt and
sadness than they are anger. Anger is extremely important in the healing process. It's a natural response to being harmed, to having your
boundaries trampled, and to being controlled and used by others for
their own purposes. Your needs, wants, preferences, feelings, opinions,
and choices were ignored and invalidated by the narcissist, while he
discounted and stomped on your identity and self-esteem. You should
be angry.

Task

If you have a hard time accessing your anger, imagine yourself when
you were three or four years old. Find a picture of yourself at that age
and look at that sweet, open, innocent face. You are the protector of
that child who still exists inside of you. Now think of things the narcissist said and did that hurt you, and imagine the narcissist saying and
doing these things to the child in that picture. Are you feeling some
anger coming to the surface? Do you feel a need to protect that dear
part of yourself? Let that anger feeling grow until you can feel it clearly.
Give it words. Write down what your anger has to say about what
happened.

Afterward, notice how the anger felt in your body. What words came
up? How do you feel about that little child self? What do you want to do
in the future to protect that vulnerable part of yourself?

Anger Is Motivating

Anger is an energizing emotion. It pushes you to action. It motivates
you to protect yourself and empowers you to move yourself away from
harm. Anger is nothing to be ashamed of. In your relationship with the

narcissist, you were exposed to his *misplaced and manipulative* anger. That is not the kind of anger I'm talking about here. You need to be in touch with your *righteous* anger. Righteous anger is a natural response to the threat of annihilation—which is exactly your situation.

Narcissists systematically try to merge you into a reflection of themselves. You were supposed to think alike, feel alike, behave alike. Your sense of self, your whole identity, was methodically being eliminated. Anger is the appropriate and necessary response in this situation. It's there to safeguard your individuality, personality, and self-esteem. By denying your anger in this relationship, you left your self-worth open to damage. Now is the time to bring back anger into the picture to push you toward taking better care of yourself.

BARGAINING, DELAYING, BUYING TIME

When you become aware of how you have been mistreated and victimized, bringing your anger and hurt to the surface, it's easy to want to push these thoughts and feelings away and just go back to how things were. After all, there were also many good things about your relationship; it certainly wasn't all bad. In fact, you may still feel some love and caring for the narcissist. Those feelings don't just evaporate instantaneously. There is much that you miss because there were also enjoyable, maybe even wonderful, times. You may be feeling guilty that perhaps you didn't do all you could to make the relationship work. This is bargaining.

It's hard to absorb this huge change in your life all at once. You need time to evaluate, understand, look back to see things from a new perspective. Narcissists encourage self-doubt. Your mind gets full of "maybe . . . what if . . . if only." Bargaining is the way we buy time to think things through and to test whether there is any option possible other than total relationship collapse.

This bargaining time also allows you to gain strength, learn new skills, think through your options, get others' opinions, build support, and in general prepare yourself to face this new reality. It is common to circulate through the feelings of denial, anger, and bargaining over and over as you get accustomed to your new life situation. Gradually the pieces put themselves together. As you consider the narcissist's behaviors from these new perspectives, your direction becomes increasingly clear.

DEPRESSION

Take Time to Grieve

Grieving is deeply uncomfortable and makes it difficult for you to want to participate in the good times that other people seem to be having. Grief is hard to do alone and yet uncomfortable to feel or express in normal social settings. You feel like a wet blanket. And you're right; many people do avoid being around others who are depressed. In addition, you can't force yourself to get through your grief quicker. Therefore, much of your grieving means being alone and often ruminating, sifting through memories, working through your hurt and anger, and probably too much self-criticism. All of this can be deeply painful.

Task

I recommend to my clients that they set aside a particular time once a day or every few days to focus intently on their hurt, anger, and worries about the ending of this relationship and relegate it to the background at other times. This can help you feel more in control and helps your mind attend to other things in between times.

Set aside a specified amount of time, perhaps fifteen or twenty minutes. Bring your full attention to your experiences, concerns, losses, and feelings. Think about just those things during this time. Identify one specific feeling or exerpience of loss and write about it in a journal or simply think about it deeply. Here are some questions for direction:

- What specifically have I lost?
- Why is this difficult for me?
- What emotional costs am I feeling as this relationship ends?
- What are the physical and financial costs for *me*? What can I do about these?
- What are all the feelings I'm having about this loss? (List as many as possible, and remember they may not all be negative.)

- What changes do I now have to face? Who can help me with these changes?
- What strengths do I have to deal with this situation?
- What do I need to learn about myself in order to feel better?
- How do I think I will feel about this loss by next year? In two years? In five years?
- What do I hope to be able to say to myself when I'm over this loss?

These questions help you turn your losses from vague, ambiguous, and overwhelming misery into concrete problems that can be approached one step at a time. This approach brings your intellect into the process to help soothe and reassure your emotional distress.

Despair

Depression is what some have called "the dark night of the soul."[2] In despair, you feel that you have lost everything, and you have no idea how you're going to cope with all the changes and decisions you're facing. You believe you don't know how to go forward, don't have the strength to continue, and have no direction. You may feel hopeless and helpless. You may be tempted to rage and storm or collapse and give up.

Despair is an incredibly disturbing experience. Yet it is something everyone has or will encounter. It can also be a deeply enlightening time of epiphany. When we feel at our lowest, we face the inevitable opportunity to get through it anyway. It's the basis of the motto for Alcoholics Anonymous—"one day at a time." You get through this moment, this hour, this day, this week, this month. Each day you find new strengths, perspectives, and possibilities. And most of us hate every minute of it.

Amazingly, despair is a healing experience. It solidifies that the past is melting away. It demands that you try something new—a new thought, a new awareness, a new answer. It leads you into final acceptance and ushers in the solutions you need.

Robbie tells of the time after her divorce when she had no job—she had formerly worked for her husband's company—had little money, and was sleeping at a friend's house on the couch. The only thing that helped her get through the days was working on her art. She found that it soothed her spirit and helped her feel she had some ability to do something beautiful. As she talked to other women who were going through losses, she shared how her collage artwork was helping her feel better. Within a year, Robbie had posted six videos about her work on the Internet and had the strong beginnings of a following of people searching to heal their grief through her art workshops.

Reach Out—Get Support

Grieving can be extremely lonely, and most of your friends and family become tired and ready to move on well before you have reached the end of your heartache. If you haven't done so before, now is the time to reach out for expert and specialized support—a therapist, a divorce recovery group, or a spiritual adviser. Although it can be difficult to ask for help, remind yourself that getting out of a narcissistic relationship is a more than average traumatic experience. It's hard for anyone to get through it without the extra encouragement, assistance, and real understanding from people who are trained to recognize and treat the mystifying emotional disability of narcissism.

This is also a good time to look deeply at the skills and tools you may need to overcome your tendency to be a caretaker. What keeps you so hyperaware of another person's pain and so inattentive and unresponsive to your own? Why are you willing to suffer and yet you can't stand it when others feel even the smallest disappointment? Do you have only a few or a great many caretaking behaviors? This is a good time to learn how to better balance your needs with those of the ones you love.

Be Patient

Remember that grieving takes time. The time it takes you to get through this can't be compared to anyone else's. Be kind to yourself in this process. Treat yourself lovingly and with compassion. Put aside your self-criticisms and think about how you would treat a dear friend going through this same kind of loss. What would you say to her or him? Say those things to yourself over and over until you truly feel nurtured and cared for.

ACCEPTANCE

Being Present

Thinking through the experiences you've been through with the narcissist can be helpful to understand the strange and crazy-making interactions. However, hard as it may seem to pull yourself away from the past, your life is lived in only the present. And, yes, the present can seem too scary to face. You thought you had everything planned and knew the direction you were going in life. Now everything is in a jumble, and your plans have disintegrated. It takes time to recover, get back on your feet, and formulate a new life plan.

You can do nothing about the past; it can't be changed because, try as you may, you can't bring the past into the present. You now know the narcissist is a person split into contradictory and divergent parts. You don't get to choose to have only the good characteristics. You don't get to choose how the narcissist will act, feel, or respond. Your only choice is how you decide to deal with the narcissist in the here and now, in this moment.

Being in the moment can give you a lot of clarity. You can be more observant and tuned in to the actual options you have available. You can adjust to what you're feeling more easily. You can evaluate your choices more effectively. Your life is about you, right now and right here. You can create a life that fits more comfortably with who you are now.

Accepting What Is

Acceptance occurs when you see clearly that there really is no going back to what was. No matter what you or the narcissist do from here on, things won't be the same. Acceptance can bring with it a feeling of depression at first because you're finally and fully feeling your loss. However, acceptance gives you the insight to move forward and create better results. It also brings a sense of freedom and relief when you aren't stuck in those unproductive persecutor/victim/rescuer behaviors with the narcissist any longer. You can be more open and honest about what you think, feel, and want to do. You now know that you are no longer responsible for anything the narcissist does. You now have options that weren't there before.

DON'T BUILD YOUR LIFE AROUND GRIEF

Facing the truth about this relationship can release your energy and attention to use on rebuilding your own life and sense of self-worth. However, you can get mired down in one or more of these grief and loss feelings for months or years if you don't remain aware of your goal— creating a new and better life for yourself.

Don't Get Stuck

Too much anger can turn into resentment, bitterness, or revenge. Or you might get locked into bargaining—especially if you are afraid of change, continue to believe you're responsible for the narcissist's feelings and actions, or expect yourself to continue keeping promises that the narcissist has broken or rejected. If you can't tap into your inner strength, competence, and self-worth, you may collapse into overwhelm and defeat. Keep aware of which feelings you are working to heal, and notice whether you are getting stuck in any of them. Get support and help if you don't seem to be moving forward.

Repression

Pretending that everything is OK, denying that you need help or support, condemning your vulnerability, or not allowing yourself to truly mourn your emotional injuries can all delay the healing of your grief and pain. They can fester and burst out in anger, fear, anxiety, or long-term depression. Then when another loss comes along in your life, the unresolved grief of this loss can increase your emotional reaction to that event. Working through your grief now can give you the strength, stamina, and confidence to handle other difficult situations in the future.

Overwhelming Shame and Guilt

Belittling yourself, criticizing and disparaging your reactions, and judging and finding fault with yourself as you grieve will create feelings of shame and guilt. Shame is especially debilitating and restricts your healing process because it essentially defines your sense of self as bad, worthless, and undeserving. The narcissist used blame and accusation to transfer his own feelings of shame onto you. Don't take on this projection from the narcissist. You are not guilty of making the narcissist say, feel, or do—anything.

FIND NEW MEANING FOR YOUR EXPERIENCES

New Understanding

The ending of any relationship can bring new understanding about yourself and the other person. The loss of your love, hopes, and dreams has been incredibly disappointing and discouraging. Being able to see and understand the facts of what was going on in the relationship can be a relief. When you see these patterns, you have a better chance of identifying and avoiding this kind of relationship in the future. As you recover, you'll discover that the grief work you have done helps you feel more grounded, sane, and resilient.

See Your Inner Strength

As your grief resolves, you'll find that you have a new awareness of your inner strength. You faced situations you never thought you could. You learned new skills and responses that have given you a greater sense of confidence. You're more perceptive and savvy. You're less often surprised and more prepared to handle difficulties that arise. You're more in tune with your values, preferences, opinions, feelings, and rights. These may be strengths that you didn't know you had before this loss.

Increased Humbleness

You've also learned that you can be deeply hurt, you can't heal the narcissist, and you can't do everything on your own. You're imperfect, you're not invincible, and you need help from others. You're vulnerable, and yet the earth didn't disintegrate. You found out you could actually handle more than you thought. You now know concretely how many people love you. Your life is continuing on and—surprisingly—even getting better. Remember that a crisis includes danger—and this has truly been a dangerous passage. It also includes opportunity. As you emerge from your grief, you'll see your abilities in a new light.

Knowing your frailties and limitations and going past them builds confidence. As you solve one challenging problem at a time, you gain appreciation for the fact that life is difficult but can be managed. You've become seasoned, experienced, less naïve, more discerning, and compassionate toward yourself and the struggles of others.

QUESTIONS FOR REFLECTION

Which feelings of grief are you experiencing presently? Which feelings are most challenging?

Who have you reached out to for help? Who else could you reach out to?

If you are feeling stuck, what do you think you need to help you move on?

What will indicate to you that you have reached acceptance?

What emotions are you becoming more comfortable with?

What have you learned about yourself in this process of grief? What do you think you still need to learn?

What new meanings and sense of yourself are you noticing?

What strengths are you developing?

9

HEALING SELF-ESTEEM

"If you feel lost, disappointed, hesitant, or weak, return to yourself, to who you are, here and now, and when you get there, you will discover yourself, like a lotus flower in full bloom, even in a muddy pond, beautiful and strong."
—Masaru Emoto

Your thoughts and *judgments* about yourself and your situation, along with the *resources* you have available, are actually more important than the *event* itself. This chapter shows you how to repair the way you look at yourself and your situation, restore your confidence in yourself, and regain well-being, strength, and motivation.

HEALING YOUR DAMAGED SELF

You Are Not the Cause

You thought the narcissist was going to make your life wonderful, and now you have found out it was just the opposite. You can probably still remember the good times, when you felt everything going just right and you were the sole focus of the narcissist's attention. That was a heady feeling—even addictive. But the narcissist has two sides, and now you are facing the other side. You always get both.

You did not cause the narcissist to idealize you, nor did you cause the narcissist's current hostility, blame, and rejection. Those behaviors are entirely under the control of the narcissist, not you. Stop, right now, taking any responsibility for the narcissist's actions. Begin paying attention to your own behaviors and focus on making choices about what you need and want to do to make your life better. Taking action helps you move out of the feeling of being a victim.

You Don't Have to Be a Victim

Even though you have been victimized by the narcissist, you don't have to feel or act like a victim. If you change the label of *victim* to the word *disappointed*, it's amazing how much this changes how you think about your current situation. When you identify yourself as a victim, you end up feeling hopeless and helpless. You tend to focus on only your pain, discounting your strengths and overlooking the people who love and care about you. You feel like giving up. You feel singled out and somehow a failure.

When you identify your feelings as disappointment, it helps you define your situation in a way that you know you can handle. After all, who hasn't been disappointed? You've coped with disappointments before and gotten over them. This may be a much bigger disappointment, but really, you are just having to make changes that you don't like and that don't fit with what you thought would happen. That is disappointment. Here are some examples:

Failure	*Disappointment*
I'm a failure at relationships.	This relationship didn't work out the way I expected.
No one will ever love me again.	I'm sad that John doesn't love me, but I know my friends and family love me.
Here I am alone again. What a failure.	It's a real setback that the relationship I counted on is over. I really didn't want this to happen.

It is hard to rebuild your life when you see yourself as a failure. It leaves you with no hope. On the other hand, seeing this experience as a disappointment, inspires you to think of the bigger picture of your life. You can see yourself more as a whole, and your experiences are just a part of that whole. It's easier when you remember that there are other people who love you, care about you, and support you. You have skills, traits, and abilities that you can use to restore your life. Seeing this event as an unwanted change, rather than as a disaster, can spur your creativity and problem-solving abilities to jump in and start responding.

Give Yourself Compassion

You're not a bad person, nor are you stupid or wrong because this relationship has ended. Nearly 50 percent of all marriages in the United States end in divorce. Surely you wouldn't label every one of those people as negatively as you're labeling yourself.

You'll improve your self-esteem immeasurably by being more compassionate toward yourself. Talk with yourself the way you would to your dearest friend if she or he were going through this same experience. What would you say to ease the pain? What words of encouragement would you give? You wouldn't be threatening, accusing, blaming, or self-righteous. Stop all these forms of self-judgment. Negative self-attacks are leftover repeats of what the narcissist has said to you. Letting go of the narcissist includes letting go of his invalidations and consciously choosing to treat yourself in a more loving and considerate manner.

Soothe Your Body

Underlying your grief are body sensations and raw emotions that actually cause pain, fatigue, low energy, and apathy. When you go through a wrenching experience, your body can become achy, tense, and jumpy, making it difficult to eat, sleep restfully, or recover from feeling continually exhausted. If you don't take care of your body's responses to all these stresses, it can become vulnerable to migraines, intestinal upsets, backaches, and even more serious ailments, such as autoimmune responses and depression.

Don't overlook good physical care. Identify your favorite, healthy foods and make sure you always have them on hand. If you're feeling angry, hard, crunchy foods can help you feel better. If you are hurting or feeling low, soft, smooth foods can be comforting. Consciously consider the foods you are eating and choose ones that make you feel good. Linda lived on shrimp for a month after her divorce. Henry chewed through two pounds of carrots and said it honestly helped relieve his anger. Be aware of high sugar foods, though, as they can lead to mood swings, which make you feel worse by throwing your body's insulin levels into chaos.

Get adequate sleep. Keep regular sleep times and have a soothing routine before bed. Even try rearranging your bedroom or get rid of the bed you shared with the narcissist if old memories keep you awake. Listen to quiet music, read, or journal. Don't spend time right before bed doing anything that will bring up thoughts of anger about the narcissist or fears about your future.

Spend time on regular relaxing routines for your body—get a massage, spend time in a hot tub or sauna, take a hatha yoga class, take time to stretch your muscles several times a day. Anger, fear, and sadness all tend to trigger muscles to tense. When you are tense, your blood flow is compromised, and you'll have trouble thinking and will tire more easily.

Exercise is one of the cheapest and most effective ways to deal with depression, anxiety, and worry. Any time your body is moving, stretching, and active, you'll feel more capable, hopeful, confident, and less pessimistic. Find a form of exercise you particularly like. Going to a class or having someone to exercise with can help motivate you to keep at it. You need your body and mind to function as well as possible as you face these changes and make decisions about what to do next in your life. Unfortunately, when you feel the worst, it can be the hardest time to treat yourself with kindness and compassion. You may think you're too tired to exercise, but take it slowly and move your body any way you can—even just a walk around the block. As you feel better physically, you'll also feel better mentally and emotionally. When you take good care of your body, your brain registers that you are worthy, valuable, and important. This is a good start to enhancing your self-esteem.

Reach Out to Others

A big part of self-esteem is based on the way friends and loved ones act toward you. How they treat you, describe you, and interact with you can have a great effect on how you feel about yourself. Because you have just come out of a relationship that was extensively based on the narcissist's warped and hostile view of you, it's essential that you get feedback about who you are from more emotionally healthy people.

Task

Think about which of your friends, family, and acquaintances are the most objective, realistic, and overall kind, and reach out to them. Spend time with them. Notice how they treat you and how you feel around them. If you've got the courage, ask some of them for feedback about how they see you. Have them write down the qualities and traits that they see in you. You could also ask for a list of your strengths and even a list of the things you need to develop, correct, or learn to handle better. Oftentimes, the people who love and care about you are just waiting for a sign from you that you'd be receptive to their assistance and support.

You may think you don't need a support group, that what you are going through is private and you can or should be able to do it on your own. However, we humans need each other for support and emotional tending when we go through difficult and painful experiences. Exclusion, shunning, and solitary confinement are the most powerful punishments there are for humans. You've been too isolated. To heal, you need to be around people. Being socially connected to other people builds up your self-esteem. When you're around people who accept and appreciate you, your healing will move along more quickly.

Self-Encouragement

The narcissist continually spent time telling you what you didn't do right, and it's likely that those messages are still playing in your mind. It takes conscious effort and attention to change these messages. You can't just push them away. You have to actively dislodge them with positive encouragement and reassurance. It always feels good when others are the ones giving you that encouragement, but someone can't always be by your side. You're the only person who is always there, so you're the best one to take on the role of encourager.

When you're afraid, discouraged, and feeling alone, it can be difficult to face all of the changes and losses you're experiencing. The next step is to figure out what feelings you would like to have instead and then develop the strength to realize them. That strength is fostered primarily by your own self-encouragement and advocacy. What you say to yourself is vitally important. You may not have been paying much attention to your own inner monologue, so start noticing now how you talk to yourself.

Do you talk to yourself as *you*, for example, "you should, you can't, you are"? This will create a sense of discouragement. It feels like someone outside of yourself passing judgment or controlling you. By making two small changes, you can start increasing your self-esteem and courage. Change "you" to "I" and make the action positive instead of negative. Start saying "I want, I can, I am." Here are some examples:

Discouraging	*Encouraging*
You have to make the bed.	I want to enjoy a clean house so I'm going to make the bed.
You should make that call to Ted.	I want to get this call over with so I can relax.
You can't get all of this done.	I can take one thing at a time.
You know you are likely to fail.	I can give this a try.
You are so stupid.	I am capable of doing what I need to do.
You are a loser.	I'm kind and considerate.

Changing what you say to yourself and how you treat yourself is the quickest way to grow your self-esteem.

Give Yourself Time

Healing a damaged self-esteem takes time and effort. The longer you were in the relationship with the narcissist, the longer it may take. Emotional and psychological change isn't a quick fix. Just like building muscle strength, it takes practice to change these old habits and internal messages. Think about building your inner self-encourager the same way you see going to the gym to build your body. Get into a routine. With consistent effort and attention, the results will be well worth the effort.

QUESTIONS FOR REFLECTION

What feels different when you say "I'm a victim" versus saying "I'm disappointed"?

How do you give yourself compassion? Who else is compassionate toward you?

How are you nurturing and healing your body? What else could you do that would be healing?

What challenges do you face when reaching out to others?

What are your most comforting self-encouragement statements?

Talk to yourself from "I" rather than "you." What do you notice?

Practice making a positive statement to yourself instead of a negative one. How does that feel?

10

REBUILDING SELF-CONFIDENCE

"Spending too much time focused on others' strengths leaves us feeling weak. Focusing on our own strengths is what, in fact, makes us strong."
—Simon Sinek, author of *Start with Why*

Self-confidence helps you have the strength and courage to tackle all the changes you are now facing in your life. When you're fearful and unsure of yourself, it's much more difficult to make the strong, positive decisions you need to make.

Self-confidence is rebuilt by changing your actions and attitudes. Having new, positive experiences helps neutralize old, bad experiences. It helps to identify your strengths, go back to doing things you love, and have an enthusiastic support team. You'll probably need to learn some new skills as well. As you take well-thought-out risks and are successful, you'll become more self-assured. However, taking risks requires that you have a positive and hopeful attitude to motivate you.

Call On Your Inner Strengths

Healing your self-esteem and rebuilding your emotional strength creates the self-confidence you need to take the risks to move ahead. To do that, you need to tune in again to the abilities you already have. Here's an exercise that will help.

Task

Make a list of your strengths and talents. Recall your childhood and adolescence and remember things you learned to do then; add them to the list. Include interpersonal abilities, such as being a good friend, loyalty, caring, and helpfulness, as well as concrete skills, such as good cook, handles finances well, good organizer. These don't have to be things you are excellent or perfect at doing—just things you are capable of doing. Now, make a list of things you've liked and enjoyed doing over your lifetime. Again, these don't have to be things you are good at. Notice where the two lists overlap. These are your strengths.

Add to these lists whenever you notice new interests and abilities. Acknowledging these strengths will help you be more courageous, capable, and able to handle difficult situations. Keep it posted somewhere as a continual reminder of who you are and what you have to offer to others, to your friends and family, and to the world. It may be easier to see your faults or failings, but focusing on those right now won't help you make headway in your healing. Keep your attention on the positives, and your confidence will grow.

Marie's list of strengths included makes friends easily, caring and helpful, former hairdresser, and good at sales. Her list of the things she liked included helping others, loves dogs, enjoys talking with people, and likes to be busy. There were other things on her list, but these were the items that came together for her when she was trying to figure out what to do with her life. She had just gotten divorced, and after being out of the workforce for over a decade raising her kids, she needed to find a job. She spent several months feeling depressed and lost. She didn't want to go back to being a beautician—too many hassles working with people who were touchy about how they looked. After making her list, Marie realized that her love of dogs and enjoyment of cutting hair could cross paths. She went to dog grooming school and is now delighted with her new job working with dogs and talking with their owners in a small dog grooming salon just down the block from her own home.

Give Yourself Credit

It also helps your self-confidence to tell others about your successes and what feels good about your accomplishments. This gives you the opportunity to receive encouragement and support. Reciting the incident and how you handled it also helps you anchor it in your memory. Instead of mulling over past upsetting events with the narcissist, take time to deliberate on your successes, your courage, and your perseverance. Keeping track of your past and present accomplishments helps you feel braver and stronger and gives you more self-assurance for the next new encounter.

People who have caretaker tendencies often find it uncomfortable to share their successes with others, despite the benefits, because they believe they're bragging or begging for attention, just like the narcissist. However, the narcissist never feels shy about sharing his successes—so this is quite different. You deserve to get credit and support from others, and it helps balance all the support, encouragement, and optimism you give to them.

Give Yourself Encouragement

Your attitude, thoughts, and self-talk have a significant influence on your self-confidence. Remember, the *Little Engine That Could* kept saying to himself "I think I can. I think I can." There are a multitude of tasks and decisions facing you as this relationship ends. You can face them with fear, anxiety, and the belief that your life is collapsing and unrepairable, or you can identify what needs to be done, ask for help, and take each problem one at a time. When you encourage yourself, you'll be less afraid. Remind yourself that hundreds of thousands of people dissolve relationships every year; you are not alone. You can get assistance, and you will get through this experience. Even if you can take only one step each day, you're still advancing.

Collect a Group of Supporters

Feeling support from others may be something you haven't experienced in a while. You're good at supporting others, but you may not feel comfortable asking for support or trusting others to give it. The narcissist said he was being supportive, but it felt like—and was—stressful, tiring, and hurtful, so you may have forgotten what support feels like.

Choosing healthy, generous friends for emotional support in your day-to-day life is entirely different than relying on a narcissist. Good friends can provide wonderful reassurance even when all you're doing is going out to lunch or playing a game of tennis. It's hard to be self-confident all by yourself. Having a group of caring and compassionate people in your life is encouraging and energizing.

Joining a support group where you can hear about and share experiences can also be validating and reassuring. Pick a group led by a professional who understands narcissists and can provide you with ideas about how to rebuild and strengthen your sense of self.

Yes, you may be facing this situation alone, but knowing there are people rooting for you and believing in you can add tremendously to your self-assurance.

Learn the Art of Reciprocity

The narcissist overvalued what he gave and undervalued what you gave. Your response was to keep giving and giving. As a result, your ability to tell whether there is a fair give-and-take is probably faulty. You may need to learn how to tell when things are mutually beneficial so you can wean yourself away from your old habits of excessive giving. One way to do that is to start keeping track of what you're giving and receiving, even though you may feel uncomfortable and selfish doing it at first. Here's an exercise to help you recalibrate your inner reciprocity calculator. With practice, it'll become more automatic. It's actually pretty simple.

Task

Start by giving time or attention to someone, and then wait until he or she gives you something of similar value before you give again. You're taking nothing away from the other person; you just aren't giving too much to start with. Keep track of what you receive from the other person, and really consider its value to you.

This exercise has two benefits. First, you pay closer attention and acknowledge what you have received, which usually feels very good. Second, you stay constantly in tune with your feelings about the relationship. Therefore, you know very quickly when or if the relationship starts feeling unbalanced. Instead of giving too much and then feeling hurt, anger, and resentment, the imbalance can be addressed swiftly—and usually more easily—right away.

For example, you want to reach out to someone you think might be a possible friend. You invite this person to lunch. If you have a good time, you say so and wait for an invitation back. You don't initiate three or four more invitations to show your interest. When you overgive at the beginning, you set a precedent for that to continue. It's also helpful to notice whether the other person is overgiving to you and how that feels. Usually it feels like an obligation or pressure. Reciprocal relationships have a balance of investment and interest. You feel more self-confidence because that balance feels supportive and reassuring.

Learn New Skills

Real self-confidence is built on knowing that you can handle both new and familiar situations effectively. It grows when you learn new skills that expand your repertoire of successful responses. It can take braveness to acknowledge that there is something you don't know but would like to learn. However, being open and willing to face new information and do new things could ultimately change many things in your life for the better. Instead of being an expert, you're the beginner. Although it takes some self-confidence to try something new, it can build even more self-confidence.

Anything new that you learn to do helps your confidence. Pick things you think would be fun, useful, and interesting. The added benefit of pursuing your own interests is that you meet new people along the way who like those same activities. Don't wait to match someone else's interests. Follow your own, and see who shows up.

Take On New Challenges

When you only do what you've always done, you'll only get what you've always gotten. If you want to move forward and grow in your life, you'll need to take on new challenges. If you start by learning a new skill, the challenges automatically appear one step at a time. Remember, you get to set the pace of your life now. The narcissist is no longer demanding or cajoling you to go at his speed and only in his direction. Choosing can be a little scary, but it can also be invigorating. Meeting new challenges develops new strengths and increases self-confidence. When you know that you can handle whatever comes along, you've rebuilt your self-confidence.

Task

Name a challenge you have faced, identify the strength you used to handle it, and write it down in a notebook. Remember how you felt going into the challenge, and reflect on how you felt after it was over. Sometimes, just having the courage to face a new and difficult situation—no matter how it turns out—is the accomplishment. Don't get sidetracked with whether you got entirely what you wanted or you did it perfectly; give yourself credit for what you learned and whatever you were able to do. Every step is an achievement, and when added to every other step, your confidence grows.

CONCLUSION

Increasing your self-confidence starts with your acknowledging and giving yourself credit for the inner strengths you already have. Add to that encouragement and support from others, and you feel your confidence and self-assurance grow. The ability to balance the give-and-take in your relationships helps you feel secure enough to reach out to learn new skills and take on new challenges.

QUESTIONS FOR REFLECTION

What are your current strengths? How can they help you face the new changes in your life?

What are your top ten talents and abilities?

What interests have you forgotten about that you might pursue again?

What encouraging statements can you use to motivate yourself to try new experiences?

Who are your supporters? Who would you like to add?

What help do you need from others? Who could you ask? What is stopping you from asking?

What imbalances do you see in how much you give and receive from others?

What new skills would you like to learn?

What new challenge are you ready for?

11

LOVING YOUR *SELF*

"Our entire life . . . consists ultimately in accepting ourselves as we
are."
—Jean Anouih, French dramatist

Whenever a significant relationship ends or radically changes, it pulls
up old memories, self-judgments, and a need to look at your life from a
new perspective. It gives you a chance to know yourself more deeply—
both your strengths and imperfections—and it challenges you to greater
self-acceptance. When you truly know who you are and love yourself
fully, you become stronger and are more willing to be open and vulnerable. Your self-esteem and self-confidence expand, and your overall life
improves. And, surprisingly, your compassion and willingness to share
your life with others also expands.

KNOW YOURSELF

A crisis such as you have been experiencing is jarring to your continuity
of self. Ordinarily you go along in your life thinking you know yourself,
know what you want and what you value. When a significant relationship ends, it's like an earthquake shaking up your assumptions and
habits. Nothing looks quite the same and nothing feels the same. What
you thought you knew about yourself becomes confused and chal-
lenged. There are new reactions, information, and demands to make
new decisions.

Embrace Your Emotional Growth

Change precipitates emotional growth. Little change happens when life is going along happily and calmly. In fact, most people don't actually like change. Advertisements disguise change by describing it as "newer and better" because we humans usually resist change, especially if it comes suddenly and not of our own choosing.

However, life, people, and circumstances are always changing. Psychological growth is often stimulated by changes that happen around and to you. If you can urge yourself to think of the change that is going on right now in your life as an opportunity for insight, growth, and personal understanding instead of as a disaster, you'll find that you can use this time to move forward spiritually and emotionally and you'll heal more quickly.

Task

Get out your journal and spend some time answering these questions. What are you learning that is truly important to you? How have your priorities changed or become more clear? Have you had emotional reactions that were surprising or new to you? What did these reactions tell you about yourself? What changes in your opinions or beliefs have you noticed? What were you previously sure about but now are questioning? What have you learned about your friends that you didn't know before? What decisions are you reevaluating, for example, choices about work, where you live, what activities you select, and how you interact with your children or parents?

You can face these changes with fear or with excitement, with dread or with curiosity. Notice what you're feeling, and be kind and gentle with yourself as you confront all these adjustments. Don't force yourself to be more positive about them than you feel. However, don't get overwhelmed with a vision of disaster. Check your feelings throughout the day. You'll notice that they change back and forth quite a bit.

Observe Without Judgment

You'll learn the most about yourself and heal more rapidly if you keep in mind to make no judgment. You can use all this new information for your benefit if you *observe* without judging whether things are right or

wrong, good or bad, likeable or not. Judgment stops curiosity and inves-
tigation. Just collect information; don't do a lot of analyzing or criticizing. This is a time to weigh and consider.

Task

Questions for your journal: What new thoughts and actions do you
notice in yourself? How are these changing and affecting how you act
and feel? Notice how others react. Give yourself time to review and
contemplate what you're learning. What new preferences do you notice? What do you want to encourage in yourself? What criticisms sneak
in?

Criticism, negative labels, and disapproval stop the learning process
and move your brain into pain and survival modes. Being calm and
relaxed encourages the collection of new information and better understanding. The end of a relationship requires that you adapt quickly to
changed circumstances. It helps to remind yourself that you're always
doing the best you can at the moment. Give yourself credit for this.

Notice Your Preferences

Living with a narcissist squashes your awareness of your own likes,
dislikes, and preferences. You learned after a while that the narcissist
wasn't going to pay attention to what you wanted anyway, so why bother
to figure it out. Therefore, you may find yourself shocked and surprised
that now there are tons of decision possibilities and you don't know
what you want. What restaurants do *you* like? What activities? What
style of decorating? What color of dishes? Which friends are really *your*
friends? How do you like to spend *your* free time? What do *you* like to
eat?

There are other more serious choices to be made as well, and you
may not yet know what you want to do about those. The narcissist can
pressure you to make decisions quickly about finances, joint property,
and the children. Try to put off any decision that doesn't absolutely
have to be made immediately. Even taking a day or a week to let
yourself think about it will help. Once you know the relationship has
ended, stop trying to figure out what the narcissist wants. This only
confuses and delays your process of determining what is best for you.
Your time and energy are better spent on determining what you want.

Making New Choices

You have a lot of new choices facing you. If you feel unsure of your wants and needs, talk about your options with people you trust not to pressure you with their own preferences and wishes. A good support person will listen, point out the positive and negative possibilities, and ask you lots of questions about how you feel. Let yourself enjoy the freedom of choosing for yourself. Take your time; notice choices that bring you enjoyment and those that don't work out. Don't condemn yourself for choices that you disliked; just make different ones the next time. Remember to look at everything as information, rather than an evaluation of yourself.

There will also be things you have to deal with that you don't choose. You may not get all the belongings you wanted or the exact schedule with your children that you preferred, or you find certain friends you counted on are no longer available. That doesn't mean you don't have choices. One of the most important choices you have to make is how you'll handle situations you don't like. Avoid seeing this as a win/lose situation with the narcissist.

You don't lose just because you don't get what you preferred. You lose when you collapse and feel devastated by it. When you let yourself feel defeated by the narcissist, you're moving back into the victim role. You essentially give up your choice about how you'll think and feel to the narcissist's control. Hold on to your right to control your own thoughts, feelings, and reactions. Go back to your values and your own life goals, and move toward them. That will take you out of the narcissist's control, and you'll find yourself more grounded and strong.

ACCEPT YOURSELF JUST AS YOU ARE

Observing without judgment leads you to self-acceptance. Emotional growth occurs as the result of encouragement, not censure or disparagement. It's easy to accept your positive and likeable parts. The real challenge is accepting *all* the parts of yourself, including the thoughts, feelings, and actions you don't like or you find embarrassing or that make you feel vulnerable. Condemnation of any part of yourself increases tension, anxiety, and procrastination. This makes change much more difficult.

Acknowledge and Accept

Acceptance does not mean that you necessarily like a certain attitude or action; it means you acknowledge it's there without condemnation or self-rejection. No one is perfect, nor should you expect to be. When you accept your imperfections and shortcomings without panic or shame, it is easier to make changes, whereas hating parts of yourself eventually leads to hating the whole self.

Much of the pain from ending a relationship is due to the belief that somehow there was something wrong with you. Self-acceptance is exactly what the narcissist cannot do. His less than perfect parts are so horrifying to him that he has to wall them off, disown them, and project them onto you. You've seen and felt the results of that method.

There is nothing wrong with you. You are not perfect, but no one is. Anyone who loves you will accept all of you. That means that to truly love yourself you will also have to find a way to accept *all* of you.

Self-Compassion

A willingness to see all of your strengths and vulnerabilities opens the door to self-compassion. You begin by applying your ability for caring, love, kindness, generosity, and deep empathy to yourself to heal your fears, anxieties, and loneliness. Self-compassion is a process of being your own best friend. You listen to your wishes, you care about your feelings, and you try to understand your wants. You care deeply and lovingly for yourself. You protect yourself. You appreciate yourself. You gently guide yourself without harsh criticism. This may take some practice and self-reminders, but the results are so enjoyable that you'll become a fan.

Self-acceptance and compassion can also shield you from the negative judgments of others, because now you own the right and the power to see and accept who you are. When you know and accept yourself, there will no longer be any fear that others will see something objectionable in you that you don't know about. Nor can anyone ever lie to you again about who you are because you know deeply the truth of yourself. You are more resilient. In addition, self-compassion ultimately frees your loving energy to expand beyond yourself to others.

Self-Encouragement

It is an entirely mistaken belief that criticism, punishment, and rejection make anyone a better person. Studies in classrooms show repeatedly that learning increases when teachers express *encouragement*, not disapproval.[1] You're probably good at encouraging others, but you may not be good at encouraging yourself. As long as you encourage others and not yourself, your self-esteem will be in jeopardy.

When you criticize other people for their negative behaviors toward you, it also decreases your own self-esteem. Criticizing others is actually a tricky way of being critical of yourself. For example, when you focus on the lies, cheating, ridicule, or selfishness of the narcissist toward you, there is an underlying subtle implication that you are unworthy, a loser, and/or powerless. It's also important to neutralize those devious self-attacks with self-empowerment statements.

Task

Use self-encouragement to take the place of self-criticism. Each time you notice yourself being critical of yourself or of others, turn the thought into an encouragement statement. Here are some examples:

Critical	*Encouragement*
I'm too fat.	I can get into better shape.
I'm always anxious and afraid.	I am willing to support and protect myself.
What's wrong with me?	I'm OK just the way I am.
She is so mean.	I don't like what she's doing. I can choose to stay away from her.
She says such lies about me.	I know the truth about who I am.
He doesn't love me anymore.	I know and love myself.
I can't possibly do that.	I have the courage to face new situations.

Notice that each of the encouragement statements is also an assertion of power and choice. The statement identifies who you are and what you can and are willing to do to take care of yourself. They are action statements. They give you direction and remind you of your path to feeling better.

Take the Pressure Off

No one likes feeling angry or hurt, and of course, you want to get over those feelings as quickly as possible. However, grief and healing take time—always more time than anyone wishes. Putting pressure on yourself to "get over it" or judging yourself for "taking too long" to heal just adds more stress and pressure, which slows down your healing. Take the pressure off yourself to meet any sort of timetable of grief and recovery. Accept that you are getting through this the best you can.

However, if you see that you are burdening your friends and family too much or you are feeling stuck in particularly strong feelings of grief or pain, it's a good time to consider working with a therapist. Often, the insight of a neutral, yet caring, professional can give you the boost you need. Find a therapist who is familiar with narcissism so you can get the most helpful information about how to deal with the narcissist in the present as well as insight and understanding about what you need to do to quit caretaking.

You Always Do the Best You Can

This statement can be difficult for many people to accept. It is based on the premise that in each moment you'll pick the best response you know at that point in time. Later, you may see a better option, but you can't take what you know now and send it into the past to change things. And you don't need to judge yourself for not knowing then what you know now or not knowing now what you'll know in the future. Life is a continuing transformation. Your ability to know and choose wisely increases moment to moment. At any one time what you say or do leads you to the next moment. If you wish you'd said or done something else, that insight can lead you to new learning and progress, so there is no need for self-criticism. Congratulate yourself on seeing that the choice didn't work or wasn't productive. Take the next opportunity to make a new choice that works better. This is awareness, and every moment of awareness is a moment of being alive and healing.

However, beware of people who constantly use the phrase "I did the best I could" as an excuse not to be responsible for their actions and who make no effort to be mindful and growing. We're always responsible for our own actions. If you are thoughtless or hurtful toward someone and you don't repair it, you're only doing the best that you are willing to do.

BE TRUE TO YOURSELF

You Are Important

Caretakers can find it hard to value themselves as important. In actuality, you're the most important person in your life. It is necessary for your self-esteem and healing to enthusiastically respond to your own thoughts, feelings, wants, and needs. Doing so is your number one job in life. If you don't take care of yourself, the only alternative is that you expect someone else to take care of you.

When you're important to yourself, you're valuing your uniqueness and contributions to others. That's not the same kind of importance the narcissist is giving himself. Narcissists want to be *more* important than anyone else. I'm suggesting that you appreciate your value and expect others around you to also respect and appreciate your value.

Knowing yourself and valuing who you are sets a standard that is communicated in your attitude, body language, and reactions to others. You're well aware that just a look from the narcissist lets you know what he expects to put up with. That's the same for you as well. What you believe about yourself and how you expect to be treated is also sent out to others in your facial expressions and body language. Your expectations and self-esteem are instantly transmitted to others by the ways you interact. When you value yourself, others get the message.

You Have the Right to Make New Choices

Have you ever wondered how you got here? Your life has evolved into what it is because of every thought, action, and choice you have made in response to the events and information you have experienced. It is important to remember that you are making new choices every single day and your choices can always change as new events and options occur. If you believe you have to stick with the first choice you ever made about something, you can really feel disheartened. Just about every choice in life can be rechosen, and you deserve as much as anyone else to choose the people, places, and activities that give you joy.

The more consciously aware you are about your choices, the more successful those choices will be. A lot goes in to making a choice that fits who you truly are. Thoughts, feelings, information, values, expectations, and goals all need to be included in the process. Too often it is just simpler and quicker to focus on only one or two of these components rather than take the time to fully evaluate what will bring you closer to what you're hoping for. This is a good time to reevaluate your past choices and see whether they are still serving you and moving you toward your life goals.

Values and Decisions

You'll find yourself happier when your day-to-day life reflects your deepest held values. Part of the way you truly know yourself is by being consciously in touch with what you find significant and important in life.

Task

Do you know what is especially important to you? Take some time to make a list of what you value. However, I want to suggest a new way to do that list. Usually, people list things such as love, honesty, happiness, and relationships, but these are huge, vague categories and aren't much help in figuring out life goals or making particular decisions. Go ahead and make your general list, but then take each category and list specific things that are important to you. Here are some examples:

General category	*Specifics*
Love	I feel loved when:
	My feelings are considered by others
	When someone is willing to help

I receive daily kindnesses, such as a cup of
coffee, encouraging words, or a hug

Honesty   I feel someone is
being honest when:

Information is
volunteered

I feel my well-being is
kept in mind

I experience others
keeping their word

Making your list specific enables you to know when these values are
actually happening in your interactions. You can then tell whether your
relationships are embodying your ethics and yearnings and moving toward your hopes and life goals. A specific list also gives you guidelines
to follow. Using your values gives you higher-quality decisions and a
greater sense of control, satisfaction, and comfort.

Quit Giving In to Make Other People Happy

It is honestly not your job to make other people happy. Anyway, it's also
impossible to actually make anyone else happy. Yes, you can offer joy
and pleasure to others through your actions, but it is entirely up to them
whether they can or will accept what you are giving. It's an amazing
consequence that when you make a happy life for yourself, the people
around you also tend to be happy people. Start from the center—happiness in yourself—and work outward sharing your happiness with others.
People who refuse or reject that gift are automatically people who don't
fit in with your values, life goals, and character. Let them go, and move
on to those who gladly accept what you have to offer.

Stop Caring About Other People's Opinions

Acknowledging all the parts of yourself—things you like and don't like,
your competent as well as your fearful and weak parts, your loving and
kind as well as your selfish parts—creates the foundation for becoming
immune to the narcissist's manipulations. When you accept who you are

completely, no one else's opinion of you is more valuable than your opinion of yourself. Critical remarks, lies, and insults no longer produce the searing pain they once did. You can then listen to complaints or comments about your behavior calmly while considering the merits of the information and the person delivering them. You are then the final judge of who you are.

When you know and accept yourself fully, then negative remarks and opinions from others no longer trigger self-attacks but can simply be used as information about the situation and the person saying them. Knowing yourself and your values creates a core of true strength and steadfastness. You're no longer easily buffeted by the changing and varying opinions of others. Your encircling group of family and friends gives you the courage to ignore the hurtful comments and anger from strangers and self-serving antagonists. There is a greater sense of confidence and composure when you reach this point.

SHARE WHO YOU ARE

Share Your Talents

One of the best ways to love and validate yourself is to share your talents and abilities with others. The appreciation you receive from people who get the benefit of your skills and gifts can go a long way toward healing your wounded self-esteem. When you contribute to the learning and betterment of someone else's life, you'll find that your old caretaking behaviors of giving advice and fixing other people's problems will more easily dissipate.

Identify what you want to share with others. This can be a huge step in valuing yourself. Decide how much time and energy you want to give, and then enjoy the giving. Do only what you truly like to do and only as long as it feels good to you to give it. The moment you trigger your sense of drudgery or resentment—stop. Keep in the spirit of giving rather than obligation.

Share Your Experiences

Let people know who you are. Share information about where you have lived, places you have traveled, stories from your past, events you've experienced, people you've known, things you like to do, and topics you find interesting. You are valuable and important, and the experiences you have had are interesting. When you've lived in the shadow of a narcissist, you can lose the awareness that you are equally interesting and worthy of being seen and heard. It may take courage at first to put yourself forward and share who you are, but it will significantly increase your self-esteem.

Share Yourself and Your Life Experiences

You are a combination of what you think, feel, do, and find curious and interesting. The most delightful and easy-to-be-around people are those who share about themselves without hostility or self-criticism and without boastfulness and superiority. If you keep your thoughts, feelings, and experiences overly safeguarded, others won't feel at ease or emotionally safe around you, fearing that you're secretly hiding something or making judgments about them. The narcissist wanted you to be invisible and your life with him concealed to protect his own image and secrets. The experience of emotional concealment can make you feel that there is something wrong with you. As you open up and just share ordinary thoughts and feelings with others, you will find a sense of freedom and a feeling of being OK just the way you are.

LOVE YOURSELF

Loving yourself comes from a mixture of knowing and accepting yourself, actively being compassionate and encouraging to yourself, following your values, and pursuing the life you really want. When you let go of trying to please others and just share your unique abilities and talents, you find that you feel more free, valued, and happy. As you appreciate and love yourself, you'll more easily move toward a life that fulfills you.

QUESTIONS FOR REFLECTION

How aware of your feelings are you from day to day? Are there any feelings that you particularly try to avoid?

How much do you criticize yourself? Take a five-minute count of the number of critical messages you give yourself. What did you notice?

What are the favorite things you like to do?

What behaviors, traits, or feelings in yourself do you believe are unacceptable?

Pick three encouraging statements to keep in mind as you go through the next week. Notice how you feel after saying them to yourself.

Do you believe that you always do the best you can? If not, why not?

How have you not been true to yourself? Are you being true to yourself now?

Which of your values have you been ignoring? What changes do you want to make about this?

How much do other people's opinions and judgments about you matter?

What talents, abilities, and experiences do you feel you are ready to share with others?

IV

Empowerment

12

BUILDING RESILIENCE

"A bird sitting on a tree is never afraid of the branch breaking because her trust is not in the branch but in her wings."
—Author unknown

Resilience is your ability to bounce back from hurtful, abusive, or disappointing events. You are in the process of increasing your resilience through the healing that you are doing now. Your level of self-respect, self-worth, ethical principles, and ability to effectively stand up for yourself all contribute to emotional resilience.

SELF-RESPECT

You Are Worthy

Feeling worthy doesn't mean that you're better than anyone else. It means that you value yourself as worthwhile to care about, care for, and protect. It also means that you take yourself and your needs seriously and you give them value and importance in your life. Without a sense of self-worth, you cannot tune in effectively to your own strengths, power, and rights, nor can you pay attention appropriately to your own needs or protect yourself. Your tendency to always put the needs of others before your own, without expecting and insisting that your needs be responded to, diminished your own sense of self-worth and made you vulnerable to manipulation and control. The needs of others are important, but so are yours. A healthy balance is needed for emotional well-being.

People will typically respect you at the level *you* allow, encourage, and expect. Notice how the people who honestly love you act toward you. How does it feel? Use this to give you valuable information about your sense of self-worth. Notice too if your internal self-messages are positive and encouraging, or if they are demeaning and disrespectful. If you think of yourself as unimportant, powerless, incapable, or a failure, you're setting the stage for others to also think and act toward you as if these things are actually true.

Task

Take a moment to make a list of things you find worthwhile about yourself. If you can't fill a page, you need to look deeper or ask others to help; then continue building that list. Then every time you're feeling critical and disheartened about yourself, read the list *out loud* to yourself as a reminder of your tangible worth in the world.

You could expand on this by asking each of your *trusted* friends, colleagues, and family members to write one thing that is worthwhile about you on a slip of paper, fold it, and give it to you. Don't look at it right away. Collect all the comments in a jar or envelope and then sit down alone and read them one by one. Because you probably won't know who wrote which one, it will be harder to discount the information. These are tangible descriptions of yourself that are recognized by others. Let them sink in.

Be Self-Responsive

How willing are you to respond to your own feelings, needs, and wants? When you ignore your own emotional self-care, you're showing an indifferent and disrespectful attitude toward your own well-being. Caring responses include asking others for help, taking good physical care of yourself, caring for your emotional needs, speaking your thoughts and feelings, and being as sympathetic to your own choices as you are to the choices of others. As an adult, you're responsible to do these things for yourself. If you don't show an interest in taking care of your needs, it conveys the message that someone should do it for you, which typically attracts controlling and dominating people.

Speak Up for Yourself

Speaking out about what you think, want, and choose to do is essential for appropriate self-respect. If you're not speaking your truth, then you're not really present and participating fully in your life and in the world. You don't have to be bossy about it. Just give your opinions and preferences when others are doing so. Instead of always deferring to others, stand up and campaign for what you want to do at least some of the time.

Others may comment on your change of behavior. Don't worry. People who see you and like you will actually be delighted to hear from you. When others know what you think, feel, and want, they are actually more comfortable around you because they know what to expect. They'll feel that you truly care and are more of a participant in the relationship and less of an observer. It actually brings you closer to others as they get to know you better.

EMBRACE YOUR ETHICAL PRINCIPLES

Follow Your Moral Compass

Everyone who has been in a relationship with a narcissist has lied, given in, or covered up the narcissist's bad or offensive behaviors to keep the relationship going. Going against your principles and what you feel is right is demoralizing to your self-respect and drains your inner strength and personal power. If you don't feel good about what you're doing, you won't feel good about yourself. When you make excuses for the narcissist, it eats away at your self-esteem.

Now is a good time to reset your moral compass and follow your true path. If something doesn't feel right, then it isn't what you ought to be doing. Don't talk yourself out of your own principles and ethical standards, and don't let anyone else talk you out of them either. The results are never satisfactory.

Identifying the behaviors and situations that have gone against your standards in this relationship can help you recenter your self-respect. Then you can be prepared to decide what actions you want to take to protect yourself from giving in to those things again. When you fully embrace your values and life principles, it's easier to stand firm on what you want and choose to do. You gain inner strength and resilience when you act from your ethical center to protect yourself. Let your standards direct you to the actions and relationships that are good for you.

Be Your Own Judge

You feel greater personal strength when you take over the responsibility of judging for yourself whether you are doing the right thing. You have the right to decide what is good for you, what you want to do, and with whom you want to be involved. Use your principles, feelings, passions, and goals to guide you into the situations and relationships that you find fulfilling and satisfying. When you decide for yourself what is best for you, you become more empowered.

Let your conscience be your guide—not your guilt. Caretakers too often make their choices based on how guilty or afraid they feel. This can pull you into and keep you in situations and relationships that are clearly not good for you. Basing your choices primarily on the needs and wishes of others is self-destructive. Remember, your number one responsibility in life is to take care of your own emotional and physical well-being, and *then* offer care to others—not the other way around. It's the same principle as on airplanes, where you're instructed to put on your own oxygen mask before you help others. It's a matter of survival.

Be your own judge in determining what you see, feel, and think and what choices you should make. This is your life; you get to choose. After all, you have to deal with the consequences of these decisions, whether you give in to someone else or you choose for yourself.

Be Around Others Who Share Your Values

It is much easier to follow your values when you're around others with the same guiding principles. Then when you feel unsure about a decision, you have others who know you well and can help you sort through your dilemma. Even then, remember that the final decision is your responsibility. Always remember to be cautious of people who try to convince you that their answer or suggestion is the only right one or pressure you to make a certain choice.

STAND UP FOR YOURSELF

Listen to Your Gut

You may fear, for good reason, that you'll be tricked again by the narcissist. Narcissists do not always go away and stay away. If things don't work out the way they wanted in their new life, they may come back and try to reengage. And if you have children together, you'll have to keep interacting with the narcissist for some time to come. How will you keep yourself emotionally strong, centered, and healthy?

Listen to your gut instead of your guilt, fear, or pity. Your gut is the center of your intuition and comes from your instincts, perceptions, and natural body reactions. It's a far more accurate method of telling you what you truly feel and want than your conscious brain. When you were with the narcissist, you had to close your gut intuition down because it was too often in conflict with what you thought you had to do or should do to please him.

A good method for staying in touch with your intuition is to tune in to your body. When you need to know quickly how you feel about something, pay attention to how your stomach and abdomen feel. Psychologists call this area of the body the second brain.[1] It can't be subverted by the "shoulds" and "oughts" that you've been taught to think are appropriate. It tells you clearly what you really want and feel. Notice any overall body signs of tension or pain as well. Is your neck stiff? Are you getting a headache? Is your lower back hurting? Emotions come out almost instantly in your body.[2] When your body is relaxed and calm, you'll feel happier, but when your gut is in distress, something is not right with your world.

Your gut is the center of your fight, flight, and freeze reactions. In caretakers, the most common response to distress is to freeze. To deal more effectively with narcissists, you've got to marshal your inner strength, which can't be done if you're in freeze mode. When situations are demanding or challenging, do you shut down and can't think of what to say and can't seem to focus your brain? That's freeze mode. When you feel instantly enraged and your mind is moving at super speed, that's fight mode. Obviously, if you just want to get away from the situation, you're in flight mode. These are all indicators that you need to protect yourself and get to a safe place so you can calm down and bring your rational thinking back online. Until you do that, you'll feel afraid, weak, and confused.

Narcissists try to push you to make quick responses and decisions. They sense when you're shut down and defenseless and choose that time to pressure or threaten you to get what they want. When your strength is drained and you're scared, your ability to think is compromised. Getting out of these fear modes allows you to marshal your inner strength, get your thinking cleared, and not cave in to these tactics.

Give yourself time to tune in to your body messages, calm yourself, and identify what you're feeling and why you're reacting as you are. Then spend some time thinking clearly about what you want. This may take minutes, hours, or sometimes days. Give yourself whatever time you need for this process and don't cave into pressure from the narcissist to respond immediately.

Task

Try this exercise to tune in to yourself before deciding on a response. See yourself standing strong and capable. Imagine everyone who loves you and supports you standing around you. What would these loved ones want for you? How can they be of help to you? What are the real limits and options that you have to choose from? What advice does your highest and best self give you? Mull over all of this information. Make your best choice from this place of strength.

Identify Your Rights

There are two important kinds of rights that you need to embrace to increase your sense of power—your legal rights and your humanity rights. If you own property or have children or legal obligations with a narcissist, you need to make sure you know your legal rights in your state. The *moment* you figure out that your partner is a narcissist, you need to consult a lawyer because at some point, you'll have conflicts with the narcissist over whatever you share.[3] If you know your legal rights, then you know where you stand, what to fight for, and what to expect. Narcissists are extremely good at trying to drain your power and emotional strength by creating mythical rights, threatening to "take everything," and making demands that aren't necessarily lawful. Knowing your legal rights can go a long way to allaying your fears, empowering you, and preparing you for the decisions you need to make.

Your humanity rights are more about your sense of emotional safety, well-being, positive regard, respect, self-worth, strength, and trust. These are things for which you rightfully get to set the standards. If you haven't clearly established your standards for these rights, then now is a good time to do so. Don't assume that everybody has the same ones. Your standards are based on your own sense of self-worth and self-respect. Definitely take time to spell out your expectations and preferences in friendships, with family, and in intimate relationships. These help you identify whether you're in a relationship that is good for your well-being and happiness.

Gerald said he wanted a relationship that felt like a partnership, in which both people shared in the decisions and the daily tasks. He liked a calm household, quiet voices, and sharing thoughts and feelings at the end of the day. He didn't like uproar, anger, or chaos. When he looked back on his marriage to Jennifer, he realized he'd gotten the exact opposite of what he actually wanted. The relationship had moved so quickly in the beginning that he was already passionately involved and committed before he genuinely knew Jennifer. He'd been in the habit of falling for women who were exciting and whose energy filled the room, even though that didn't match the kind of life he wanted to live. After divorcing, he decided to go slower in the next relationship and look for someone who enjoyed the same kind of lifestyle he was comfortable with. That led him to thinking about Nina, who had been a friend for years. They've been together for a decade now, deeply appreciating their quiet life together.

Clarify Your Obligations

As an adult, you have the right to choose what you will and won't do for others, how often you want to do these things, and in what way. Just because the narcissist called you selfish and accused you of not doing enough for him doesn't mean that it was true. You'll feel stronger and more empowered when you decide for yourself what obligations you choose to take on and what you expect in return.

Obligations are reciprocal, for example, parent to child and child to parent, husband to wife and wife to husband, employer to employee and employee to employer, or friend to friend. Your self-worth increases when you hold others to the same standard of meeting obligations to which you hold yourself. So when you fulfill your commitments and the other person doesn't, you've got the right to choose whether you'll continue the relationship, terminate your promises to the other person, or get help and support to enforce your rights.

Obligations freely chosen reduce the likelihood of resentment and bitterness and increase positive connections with others. Keep working to find enjoyable reciprocal relationships, and you'll find your feelings of integrity, self-worth, and strength increasing.

Kendra, age thirty-four, had learned not to tolerate her father, Danny's, narcissistic control and dominance. However, her mother was more passive and constrained by him. When her mother was diagnosed with end-stage cancer, Kendra wanted to take care of her, but she didn't want to deal with her father's demands, control, and temper tantrums. She tried to convince her mother to leave him and come live with her, but her mother didn't have the strength to stand up to Danny. So she stayed. Kendra told her mother that she would visit only when her father wasn't there but that her home was open if her mother ever wanted to live with Kendra. Danny hated taking care of his wife and complained continually. Kendra lived four hundred miles away, but drove down to care for her mother one day a week to relieve her father, but only if he was not in the house.

Her mother rallied, and she and Kendra took a trip together to Paris without Danny. When they got back, her mother was hospitalized again with a relapse. Danny threw his hands up in frustration and refused to visit his wife "because she just keeps getting worse." He moved out a week later. Kendra nursed her mother for the next two months until she died. Kendra clarified her obligations and boundaries at each step of her mother's illness and knew she had done the best she could for her mother while staying clear of her father's injurious anger and attacks.

Make Your Own Choices

When you clearly and consciously make your own choices, you'll feel stronger, more competent and powerful, and happier. Conversely, giving up what you want in order to keep others from complaining and whining will cause you to feel insignificant and resentful. When you always just go along with what others choose, you can end up believing that you don't have choices. This dilutes your strength. Even when the options are not what you would like, make a choice. You'll feel better and more in control of your life. Kendra used a self-talk exercise to help her figure out what to do about her mother and father. Following is the process.

Task—Talk Yourself Through Challenges

In an article titled "The Voice of Reason," Pamela Weintraub states that experiments done by psychologist Ethan Kross indicate that "how people conduct their inner monologues has an enormous effect on their success in life."[4] She outlined three steps that are especially effective in being more courageous and successful in difficult or challenging situations. They are (1) speak to yourself in the first person, (2) give yourself specific instructions, and (3) affirm that you are capable.

1. Speaking to yourself in the first person means using your first name to talk to yourself as if you were talking to a friend. This helps you see yourself more objectively. You can remind yourself of your past successes and ask yourself questions about feelings and thoughts. This gives you the sense of having a good friend to talk with.
2. Giving yourself specific instructions can include reminders to keep calm, instructions about what to do and say, and even directions about what feelings to have. This is reassuring and encouraging and keeps your conscious brain engaged and in charge. As a result, your mind is more able to override your fight, flight, or freeze reactions. It helps you create a plan, decide what you are going to do, and encourage yourself to do it.
3. Affirm you are capable. Continue talking to yourself using your first name. State all of the strengths and abilities you have that can help you get through this difficult situation. Avoid saying

fearful, negative, or disaster-vision self-comments. Be encouraging.

After you get through the challenging encounter, be sure to identify what was successful and the specific strengths and actions that were helpful to you. This will increase your ability to meet the next challenging situation.

Here's an example from Sondra, who calls herself Soni, encouraging herself:

> (1) Soni, what are you anxious about? You've talked to Mike [narcissist] hundreds of times before. (2) Keep breathing, look him in the eye, and tell him no. He can't hurt you anymore, Soni, unless you care what he thinks about you. And you don't care what he thinks anymore. (3) You are strong and capable, and you have the right to say no. It's OK to be yourself and tell him what you want.

Then afterward:

> Soni, you got through it. You stood your ground, and he backed off. Good for you. You are really getting strong. You go, girl.

This step-by-step process is extremely powerful and effective. You can use it whenever you face anxiety-producing situations at work, with family and friends, and especially with narcissists. It gives you the inner sense that you're twice as strong because you're there doing the actions and also there encouraging and cheering yourself on.

CONCLUSION

Being resilient includes respecting yourself, seeing your own worth, knowing what you think and feel, identifying and following your own values, and believing that you have the right to evaluate your own. To do these things, you have to listen to your deep emotional responses and honor them when deciding what to do. You also need to identify your rights, stand up for them, and take over making your own choices. Learning a new, more empowering way to talk to yourself is key. Strength and trust in yourself grow when you listen to your feelings and needs, take charge of making your own choices, and let yourself be authentically you.

QUESTIONS FOR REFLECTION

Rate your sense of emotional strength and power from 1–10 during your relationship with the narcissist. Also rate it before and after the relationship. What do you notice? How would your loved ones rate it?

What would you change if you listened to yourself more?

How well do you follow your own values and conscience?

Spend a whole day tuning in to your "gut." What does it have to say?

What do you need to do to better protect your legal rights?

In what situations do you feel your emotional safety, respect, or self-worth are being damaged? What can you do to feel more empowered?

Are you freely choosing what you want to do for others? What obligations would you like to give up?

Take a challenging situation in your life and use the steps outlined to talk yourself through it in a new and more powerful way.

13

SELF-PROTECTION

"You've always had the power . . . you just had to learn it for yourself."
—Glinda, the Good Witch of the North, from *The Wizard of Oz*

CREATING SELF-PROTECTION

When someone else is in charge of protecting you, it comes with a price. That price is control. Narcissists often describe their love as protecting you, when in fact it is aimed at organizing your life, directing and commanding you to do things their way, and monitoring your actions. When you were under the control of a narcissist, it was difficult to set boundaries and limits to protect yourself. As your self-esteem and self-confidence grow, you'll feel stronger and more righteous in protecting your emotional and physical self from anyone who would try to take control of your life again.

Stop All Personal Interactions

Some narcissists cut off contact with you, but more frequently they keep hanging around trying to get your attention, as well as dominate and manipulate you to get what they want. They continue their push/pull behaviors. It's in your own best interest to stop any sort of *personal* interaction with the narcissist. If you have business that needs attending to, try to do it through your lawyer or through short messages, with as little direct contact as possible. Any time you are friendly and accommodating to a narcissist, he's likely to think you're willing to give in to whatever he wants. When you give in to small things, the narcissist increases his attempts to get his way.

Set Limits

Figure out how to limit or eliminate your contact with the narcissist as much as possible. Arrange child drop-offs and pickups at school, sports practices, or in a public place. Use online calendars for messages and scheduling information. Don't attend the same social functions. Message or call only when absolutely necessary, and limit its length. If the communication isn't about legal matters, it probably doesn't need to happen. Don't go into explanations of why you think or feel as you do, don't expect empathy or consideration, and never change the terms of your agreements with the narcissist except by going through the legal system. As your kids get older, let them negotiate more for themselves about what they want with the other parent.

You may need to use a lot of self-encouragement when setting new boundaries and limits. The technique outlined in the last chapter can give you courage to stand your ground, say no, walk away, hang up the phone, or refuse to get triggered into a fight with the narcissist. State clearly and powerfully what you want, and follow through on any consequences you've chosen. When you believe in your rights, know what you truly feel, and have thought through what you want, you can create an effective action plan. Using the self-talk method increases your courage to stand your ground. Then this becomes a powerful self-protection system.

Hold Your Boundaries

With narcissists, you not only have to set your boundaries, but you also have to defend and continually hold on to them. Narcissists are completely focused on getting what they want, so they'll keep pushing your limits until it's clear that you're never giving up. Making exceptions or giving in "just this once" usually makes it more difficult to hold your boundary the next time. Your rights and well-being are best protected by making your statements and agreements with the narcissist clear, precise, and in writing and not making concessions later. Flexing your agreements to accommodate the narcissist's immediate wants or needs is a risky business. You can't count on the narcissist to reciprocate in kind.

Pick your battles and don't fuss around with the small things. Do as much as you can to protect yourself and your children from actual harm, but don't spend time and energy fighting battles over things that won't matter in ten years. Save your energy for the significant issues that have long-term effects.

Collect Your Allies

You'll find that you feel stronger and safer when you have loving, caring, supportive people around you whenever you have to encounter the narcissist. Narcissists are nastiest when it is just the two of you, but they're more likely to be civil when there are witnesses who support you. In social situations, sit with your friends between you and the narcissist. Be polite, but don't encourage friendly interaction. That's not necessary. You're not going to be long-term friends with someone who has treated you as badly as the narcissist has.

If you have legal issues with the narcissist, have your lawyer with you when you have important issues to discuss. Don't try to settle things on your own. This will protect you from a lot of bickering and haggling that can be exhausting and mind crushing. Ask your therapist for information and insight about what to expect. Practice with him or her for upcoming interactions. Ask your friends for moral support, and even request them to be present during your contacts with the narcissist. Allow family to encourage and support you through these times. Always aim to keep yourself calm, centered, and protected whenever you have to be around the narcissist.

However, as Jean McBride says in her book *Talking to Children About Divorce*, remember, your children should not be your allies.[1] It is harmful when you try to get them to be on your side, love you more, or tattle on the narcissist. Their relationship with the other parent is entirely different from your relationship with him or her. Also, don't try to control your children's feelings. Choose adult allies who understand your dilemma and are helpful in supporting your self-esteem and self-confidence.

Say No and Mean It

Your best protection against a narcissist is your ability to say and mean no. You can use the word specifically as in "No thank you," "No, that won't work for me," or "Not now," but you can also convey no by identifying the differences between you and the narcissist, for example,

- "You seem to want to talk more about this, but I don't."
- "Unless you stop shouting, I am hanging up the phone." (Then do it.)
- "I would like to meet in my lawyer's office rather than at my home."

When you disagree with the narcissist, make sure it's worth the effort it will take to defend your decision. Be aware that it takes a lot more energy to defend a no when you are waffling and actually mean maybe. When you're unsure, you are fighting within yourself as well as with the narcissist. A solid no is much more clear because then you know you have genuine reasons and support to back it up. You're of one mind, and that is much stronger.

You don't have to go along with the narcissist anymore, but it wastes your energy to disagree just because you're angry. Yes and no are strongest when they are well thought out and chosen in coordination with your deepest intentions and goals.

Step Out of the Game

One of the most powerful and self-protective tools you can use to shield yourself from the negativity of the narcissist's behaviors is to disengage. Whether you or the narcissist has ended this relationship, you may be surprised at how much contact the narcissist still wants to have with you. He may continue to engage you in endless e-mails and texts, or even offer to date again or be friends, or want to talk with you about his new love relationship. On the other hand, the narcissist's bid for your attention may be primarily hostile, with demands to talk things out or accusations. He might even try to push his way into your home and demand to take things. However, you'll probably face a combination of these approaches.

It's time to end the drama and step away from the game. As long as any part of you still contemplates reuniting, the narcissist has power over your feelings, thoughts, and choices. A clear ending in your mind needs to be reached before you can move on. Only then can you truly get yourself emotionally out of this drama and protect yourself from further pain. As long as you have grudges, resentments, demands, or expectations of the narcissist, you have not let go of this relationship. You may say you are done and it's over, but as long as the narcissist can make you crazy, you have not completely let go.

Some things that your former partner does will never be to your liking, but the goal is to let him go and focus your attention on the events and happenings in your own life. Don't let the narcissist continue to control your thoughts or how you feel and live your life months and years after the relationship has ended.

When Leanne came to therapy to deal with her continued anxiety and depression about her divorce from five years earlier, she wasn't aware of how much time and energy she was spending interacting with her former husband, Ron. She was sending and receiving numerous texts and e-mails daily. They had two children in high school, who were both hesitant to speak up to their dad and tell him what they wanted. Leanne always seemed afraid of Ron. He was clearly narcissistic and definitely was persistent in pushing for what he wanted.

In therapy Leanne learned to quit giving into all the minute changes that Ron wanted. She had her lawyer send him a letter reminding him of their original parenting agreement, and she quit responding to his requests for changes. When the kids wanted to do special things on Dad's parenting time, she coached them to work that out with him. Within six months, the number of communications between Leanne and Ron had decreased 80 percent, and Leanne's anxiety was greatly reduced. She even found time and energy to do social activities when her kids were with their dad, because she was no longer worrying about what would happen next.

It's OK Not to Care

It is definitely OK not to care about the narcissist any longer. You broke up. You need to let go of any nonlegal expectations and obligations. Caretakers like to "care" about other people. It may feel disloyal to you to say you don't care. Do you still have unconscious hopes that the narcissist will somehow care for you, due to your past relationship with each other? If you still have these hopes, you'll remain vulnerable to the hurtful and crazy-making interactions the narcissist has done in the past.

To truly disengage, you have to move to a more neutral place of acceptance of the narcissist and yourself as two *separate* people, *unattached* to each other. What he does or doesn't do has nothing to do with you anymore. Ignore any morbid interest you have about his current life. Let your past dreams of what you were going to do together float away. Turn your back on the past, and move forward to create a new life for yourself, full of new dreams, new people, and new experiences.

TRUSTING YOUR WINGS

Keep Your Own Counsel

No one is more motivated to respond to your needs and be a good protector and guide than you. You have the potential to know better than anyone else what you feel, think, want, and enjoy. So you're ultimately the best judge of what is good for you and what choices would be best for you. Being mindfully aware of yourself does take time and energy, but it has huge payoffs. When you know yourself and make well-considered choices, your life works much better, with less drama, fewer wrong turns, and more satisfaction. Take time every day to tune in to yourself. Listen to your thoughts, sense what feelings are coming to the surface, and give yourself permission to follow your own sense of what gives you contentment and well-being, whether or not it pleases others.

Task

Take time to be alone with your thoughts with no other distractions. Whether you call this time meditation, prayer, contemplation, or just relaxation, it is essential for your well-being. Surprisingly, even five to ten minutes a day can make a huge difference in the quality of your life. Listen to quiet instrumental music, journal, take a walk alone, or sit in nature with no agenda except to listen to what is going on inside of you. At first, you may feel fidgety or have trouble getting your mind off the many things you have on your to-do list. Take a deep breath, relax your shoulders, and give yourself permission to take a few minutes for yourself. Tell your mind that you're willing to listen to whatever it has to tell you at this moment. Then just notice what passes through your attention. Write down your thoughts and feelings if you would like. Do this for a week, noticing what patterns of worries, judgments, or thoughts keep surfacing.

These few minutes focused on yourself can be the most valuable time of your day. You become aware of your mood changes, passions, wishes, and fears. It gives you a heads-up for what you need and can expect from yourself for the next twenty-four hours. When you respond without criticism to what your emotional system needs, you can count on yourself to be your own best advocate in life. You know you can fly even if the branch breaks or the unexpected happens.

Be Your Own Authority

You might not have noticed that you're the only one who makes choices for your life, and you're the only one ultimately responsible for what you choose to do. That makes you the definitive authority over you. No matter who else has an opinion about you, your life, or your actions, it is you who ultimately makes every choice. If you believe in your own authority to run your life, you'll never again get caught up in the delusion that someone else *makes* you do anything. Nor will you fall victim to the imaginary belief that you've *caused* anyone else to feel or do anything. You'll be able to stand solidly on your own values and integrity and no longer feel like a pawn in someone else's life drama.

Let Your Authentic Self Be Your Guide

There is great joy in being authentically yourself. It gives you a sense of freedom and confidence that nothing else can. Knowing that you are plenty good enough lets your whole self be relaxed and no longer on guard. You don't have to figure out what other people want you to be. When you're being yourself, you can be assured that people who like you are accepting you for just being you. It takes tons of energy to assess and align your every action to meet the expectations of others. It takes little or no energy to just be yourself.

However, authenticity doesn't mean saying or doing anything and everything that comes into your mind, such as criticizing others, or doing anything you want without consideration for how it affects others. You don't have control over other people, but you may have a powerful influence on them. Be as respectful of the individuality of others as you would have them be toward you. Even when you stop caretaking others, you still can and will be caring of other people. However, you won't be pleasing them at your own expense.

Being authentic means knowing who you are and sharing that genuinely with others. It means being truthful about yourself, your feelings and wants, without discounting anyone else. Authenticity means that you won't cover up or discount your needs and wants just because someone else doesn't approve. It also means you don't have to give in and then feel resentful, go along with behaviors that you don't like, or pretend you have feelings that you don't have.

An additional benefit of being authentic is that you'll quickly find out whether other people are dependable, trustworthy, and genuine. Because you aren't spending huge amounts of energy trying to please other people, you'll be better able to see when people are disapproving, judgmental, and dissatisfied as well as when they are being honest, truly caring, or genuinely concerned about you. Their behaviors will be more visible, and this gives you more information to assess whether *you* like them.

CONCLUSION

Self-protection means setting limits on what you will and won't tolerate from others and what you will do and not do for them. It takes practice to hold to your boundaries, but you can do this more effectively with the help of your allies, the ability to firmly say no, and your willingness to step out of the narcissist's games, because you no longer care what the narcissist thinks about you.

Trust in yourself develops as you listen to yourself, accept your feelings and needs as normal and valuable, take charge of making your own choices, and finally let yourself be truly and authentically you.

QUESTIONS FOR REFLECTION

What interactions with the narcissist can you quit doing?

What new limits would you like to set in your life?

What limits and boundaries need your attention to make them stronger?

What things would you like to say no to?

How do you still get caught up in the narcissist's manipulations? What can you do differently?

Can you describe your authentic self?

How would your life change if you were willing to be more authentically you?

14

BECOMING INDEPENDENT

"No price is too high to pay for the privilege of owning yourself."
—Friedrich Nietzsche

You are either in control of yourself or you allow someone else to be in control of you. In the relationship with the narcissist, most of the time the narcissist was in control. As a caretaker you primarily accommodated the narcissist's feelings and preferences and deferred to his choices. Although that was quite restrictive and often exasperating, it can be difficult to automatically switch into being independent and self-reliant. Making your own decisions takes thought, time, and energy, and it can be scary to feel responsible for everything in your life again. Learning to be independent can feel lonely and intimidating. However, if you want to avoid narcissistic relationships in the future, your chances are much better if you have a clear sense of your right to be a self-determining, independent person.

Letting Go of Codependence

The relationship between you and the narcissist was codependent, whether you realized it at the time. You tried to please and take care of the narcissist, while he tried to get his way in everything. That was continually to your disadvantage. To have a strong partner relationship, both parties must be able to articulate what they want and at the same time respond to and care about the other's feelings and needs. Otherwise, the relationship will be codependent.

Speak Up for Yourself

It can be very hard to speak up in interactions with narcissists. They don't listen well and often respond to comments with hostility and derision. Caretakers want to smooth over any discord, so they back down and give up pretty easily. In addition narcissists try to turn comments they don't like back on the other person. Add in the fact that narcissists always have to be right, superior, and in control of everything, and the result is that anyone actively engaged in a long-term relationship with a narcissist will become codependent over time.

To regain your sense of independence you have to rediscover your voice. Your ability to share what you think and feel, set boundaries, make your preferences known, and stand up for your rights all depend on your being able to speak up for yourself. You may need to start by writing down your thoughts, observations, opinions, and likes and dislikes in a journal. Put words to what you are feeling and experiencing. Then pick your safest friend or family member to share these words of truth you have discovered. Allow yourself to ask for what you want, give your opinion, select the movie or restaurant you go to, and say no once in a while. Speaking up is the difference between being a wallflower or joining the dance.

The sooner you speak up and make your requirements and desires known to others, the sooner needy, selfish, self-absorbed people fade away because they quickly realize that you aren't going to be giving them what they want. Doing this saves a lot of time by narrowing the field to more egalitarian, independent, less-controlling people, whether acquaintances, friends, or companions.

Respond to Your Own Needs

As a former caretaker, you have wonderful skills for instantly and effectively responding to the needs, wishes, and feelings of others. You're probably not nearly as good at being self-responsive.

How well do you take care of your physical needs? If you have chronic physical stress, pain, low energy, or lack of joy, you need to pay more attention to your physical needs. Common physical issues for caretakers are migraines, neck and back pain, indigestion, irritable bowel, muscle tension in the jaw, fatigue, and lethargy. These are all indicators of overstressing your body with anxiety, emotional pressure, worry, guilt, and fear without respite care and recovery. What does your body need from you to recover to its full level of health? Excuses of not enough time or money to take care of yourself won't make you feel better. Take charge of caring for your health and well-being right now, and make it a lifelong priority. Without a healthy body, you'll find everything in life is more difficult.

Continue working on responding to your emotional needs with positive self-talk, self-validation, and encouragement. Make these automatic habits in your life. Rebuild your trust in yourself by being more authentically you. These things give you the strength to be more emotionally independent in your intimate relationships.

Financial independence is also important. When you know you can take care of yourself financially, you never again have to feel helpless to leave an abusive, insulting, or hard-hearted relationship due to no means of supporting yourself. Additionally, if you want to go back to school, start a business, or attend an event that interests you, you know that you have the ability to finance this yourself instead of relying solely on someone else to give you permission and the funds. As you've just experienced, being faced with living on your own is much less stressful when you can pay your own rent and buy food. Money of your own gives you choices.

Create a Vision and Follow Your Passion

Do you know where you want your life to go? Where you want to live? How you want to spend your days? Have you identified your purpose? People who have been caretakers have often lost their sense of life direction and passion. "Saving your relationship" may have been your most recent life goal. It's time now to create new life goals. As you have learned, latching onto someone else who will take you along toward his life goals is chancy and unreliable at best. On the other hand, having no goal at all almost assures that you won't get where you want to be.

Task

As you heal and become more independent and resilient, this can be a
time to create a new life plan. This is your life. What do you want to do
with it? What interests you? What excites you? What would you like to
be known for? Create a plan to move in the direction of your yearnings.
And be sure to figure out what kind of people you want to have travel
that path with you. Being choosy about your life companions isn't elitist
or selfish; it's just plain good sense. For a specialized job, you wouldn't
hire just anyone who happened to come through the door. Be at least as
choosy about the people with whom you select to share your most
intimate self.

Invest in Yourself

Pay attention to yourself. Time spent being with yourself provides your
greatest opportunity to learn who you are and create the life you truly
love and enjoy. When you're coming out of such an intense, enmeshed
relationship as you've been in with the narcissist, you may find it difficult to be alone. You may feel lonely and lost. The thought of spending
time just thinking about yourself may seem pointless, self-indulgent,
and a waste of time. In actuality it is your greatest investment in yourself.

According to essayist William Deresiewicz, "solitude enables us to
secure the integrity of the self as well as to explore it."[1] You may shy
away from time alone without the television or your phone close at hand
to provide noise and "connection." However, don't these devices frequently make you feel more lonely? Loneliness doesn't come from being alone but rather from feeling the loss of being truly known and
accepted. Weren't you lonely much of the time in your relationship with
the narcissist?

Task

Be brave and make time to sit quietly, doing nothing, and experience
being alive. This feels especially good done in nature. Sit by a lake, walk
in the woods, breathe in the air, feel the sun on your back. Allow
yourself to experience your bodily sensations and emotions. You're the
person you can count on to always be there, always be available to listen

and to care about you more deeply than anyone else. See yourself in your mind's eye—strong, contented, and confident. Remember the last time you felt this way. What was your life like then? What would it take for you to feel that way again? What hopes and dreams do you have? Think of a sentence that embodies this feeling of strength and independence, and say it to yourself. Remember it, and use it for encouragement.

When you are your own best friend, you're self-possessed—that is, you possess yourself. You're independent of the passing moods and opinions of others. You'll find a deeper sense of well-being and security when you know that you can always count on yourself.

TAKING CARE OF BUSINESS

Go for Your Goals

When you're independent and know what you feel and want, you're free to explore new ambitions, purposes, and goals. Some of those goals may be things you wanted to do from years past, and others may be new and surprising.

Task

This is a good time to create a bucket list. Write down as many things as possible that you might like to do. Listing twenty, thirty, or even fifty items allows your mind to float free and be creative. You don't have to commit to doing anything on this list. It's just for fun. For instance, "seeing the South Pole" is on my list. I really don't want to go there, but I love pictures and documentaries of that vast and beautiful land. Let your fantasy soar. Open to yearnings and aspirations that you didn't previously consider.

Look over your list and see whether there are any patterns or groups of things that appeal to you. Notice which items get you excited and energized. Then start prioritizing. Select your top ten favorite or most interesting choices, and ask yourself these questions. Which items could you do right away? Which ones will take some planning? Which things would you want to do alone? With whom would you want to share these experiences? Keep working with your list until you come up with your top three choices. When you're ready, start a planning sheet for each of these. From this process, you'll find that goals naturally develop and now you've found some possible new adventures.

Feel the Fear and Do It Anyway

If you are not used to having goals and directions, you may find a flood of emotions as you contemplate these new possibilities—excitement, enthusiasm, anxiety, overwhelm, and just plain fear. The most common fears are contradictory, such as fear of *failure* and also the fear of *success*. No one wants to fail, but the possibility of success also offers challenges that can be scary too. Either way you're going to learn a lot more about yourself.

Failure is not the same as being unsuccessful. Failure is a thought or an evaluation of lost value or merit. Being unsuccessful is simply a fact and is rarely total. Some part of anything that you do is going to be successful. It just didn't turn out completely the way you wanted or expected. Post-It Notes are the result of an unsuccessful experiment. The 3M Company was looking for a new kind of glue and ended up with this less-than-effective semisticky substance. Figuring out what to do with the results turned the catastrophe into an amazingly useful and lucrative product. Not succeeding at what you expected simply means that you've learned something, which applied creatively, might eventually make your life better.

Fear of success is harder to visualize. It is correlated to procrastination, hesitancy, not feeling deserving, and believing you're not good enough. Fear of success is evident when you worry about what you'll have to live up to or be called on to do next. For example, I've heard past caretakers say "If I did find someone who is truly loving and kind, I'm not sure I'd know how to act." You've probably heard that the most difficult thing to have happen is not getting what you want, and the second most difficult is actually getting what you asked for.

Taking the labels of failure and success off the table can make your life more agreeable and greatly reduce your fears of the future. Everything works out as it does. You have some power and influence about how things happen, but you are never fully in control of anything. Life is an improvisational dance moving this way and that. As Tina Fey points out in her book *Bossypants*,[2] the first law of improvisation is saying yes to what you've been given, and then being creative. Yes, I'm getting divorced; what do I choose to do now? Yes, I have to move out of my home; where would I like to live instead? Yes, I can no longer be on the life path I chose ten years ago; what path do I want to choose now?

Problem-Solving Techniques

Life is full of problems and new experiences that require choices and decisions that are going to bring up more problems that you don't *yet* know how to handle. Problems feel the most overwhelming when they're vague and require you to change in some way that you're not familiar with. Here are some steps that will help.

Clarify the problem. First, is it even your problem? Identify why and how the problem affects you. It's easy to get overinvolved in what other people need and how other people should be acting. If a problem doesn't directly affect *you*, reassess whether it is your problem to solve. Second, put the problem into one sentence so you can see it clearly. Third, specify the goal you wish to achieve. This'll help you move from a vague, uncomfortable situation to a specific issue.

Visualize getting from the problem to the solution. Let your mind move through different paths from the problem to the solution you want. Keep rearranging the possible actions and reactions until you find one that you like or can live with. This will help generate new ideas. Let yourself think outside of the standard, expected actions and even play with silly solutions. With each possible scenario, assess the realistic results of how you would feel and how others might respond so you don't waste too much time on "magical solutions," which require you or others to suddenly change personality or character.

Break up the problem into steps. When you have one or two solution scenarios that you think have a real possibility of working, break up the problem into steps along the solution path. Three to five steps make a good start.

Identify the skills needed at each step. Make a list of your current skills that will be needed to reach your goal. These include personal abilities, such as internal strengths, interpersonal skills, past successes, and specific talents and proficiencies.

Then identify any skills or techniques you'll need to acquire to solve this problem. Work on acquiring these skills only if they're truly necessary to reach your current step or goal. Don't get sidetracked by demanding so much that you get discouraged or another problem is created, for example, "I need to learn how to use positive self-statements instead of self-criticism," *not* "I have to get over being depressed."

Recognize and collect your resources/supports. Who can you call on to help you with this problem? That includes friends, family, professionals, groups, and organizations that have abilities you need, as well as any resources and expertise that you can call on for assistance. Information from classes, workshops, and the Internet can be collected. Figure out how much time you need to devote to this problem and how much money you can and need to bring in to help.

Create optimal functioning. What helps you operate at your best? Various strategies may be helpful, such as thinking confidently, using a positive attitude, avoiding distractions, taking breaks when you need them, working with a partner, selecting a supportive environment, and being persistent. When you know and accept your strengths and weaknesses, you can create a working situation where you can do your best.

So how do these problem-solving steps work together? Here's an example.

- Clarify problem—I want to exchange the children with my former spouse without letting him in my house and without a fight.
- Visualize—I see myself calm, standing on the porch waving good-bye.
- Steps—I'll do the exchange on the porch. I'll have the children and all of their belongings ready and waiting. I'll smile and say hello. I'll keep my voice calm and not make extra conversation. I'll stand in front of the door until they all leave. I'll then go inside and shut the door.
- Skills—I have the right to decide who enters my home. I have the ability to breathe and calm myself. I can choose what I talk about. I can remind myself that I don't have to agree or respond to any negative comments. I can refrain from being defensive by not talking.

- Resources/supports—I'll ask my friend, Sarah, to be at the exchange with me. I'll call my brother, Josh, and ask him to remind me that I'm not alone and that I'm strong.
- Optimal functioning—I'll say encouraging words and reminders to myself before the exchange. I'll be prepared to say no if he asks to come in. I'll make sure that Sarah is here well ahead of time. I'll ask Sarah to nudge me if I start to say something negative or defensive.

Review Your Success

The first time you deal with a particular situation or problem is almost always the hardest. Each time you confront it, however, you have another chance to improve your action plan and responses. The more positive and encouraging you can be with yourself, the easier it'll be to deal with the situation the next time. When you look back on how you handled things, give yourself credit for every step and goal that you accomplished. Then let yourself look at what didn't go as well as planned and consider, without any criticism, what didn't work so you can create a plan to deal with that the next time. Watch that you don't ruminate on the negatives, but instead keep focused on your new plan and visualize your success.

TRUST YOUR DECISIONS

Rely on Your Intuition

How often did your feelings tell you that things didn't seem to be working well in your relationship, but when you brought up your concerns, the narcissist responded with denial, charm, and then blame and hostility? Still, your intuition told you something wasn't satisfactory. Not trusting your intuition led you down the path to some skewed thinking and resulted in decisions that you may be regretting at this time. You may have ended up thinking that you were crazy, or too needy or selfish, or totally mistaken in what you saw, heard, and felt. Don't ever let someone talk you out of your intuitive feelings again.

Intuition is a subconscious ability to put together miniscule bits of barely observable body language, tone of voice, and emotional reactions and read those automatically and instantaneously to form an impression of what is happening around you. It's especially useful in social interactions and to alert you to emotional or physical danger. People who have high empathy tend to be excellent intuitive responders.

As you disengage from the narcissist, you've probably concluded that your intuitive feelings about certain situations with the narcissist were, in fact, accurate. Even though you aren't always *consciously* aware of why you feel certain things, don't discount those reactions. Trust your intuition. Then gather enough information and facts—not just what other people tell you—to verify or refute what you feel. After that, if your feelings are still going with your first reaction, rely on that response. The vast majority of the time, your intuition will prove to be correct.

Decide for Yourself

You may have thought the narcissist made all the decisions in your relationship, but in fact you participated in every one, often by giving in repeatedly. Perhaps you were trying to be nice, or keep from fighting, or save the relationship. However, it was actually a delaying tactic that kept the real issues out of sight without settling them. You have the responsibility to make decisions for yourself. Being in a relationship or being married does not eliminate that responsibility. If your spouse cheats on your income tax and is caught, you have to pay the penalty too, even if you didn't agree with the choice. If he alienates your children, then you don't get to see them or be as close either. When you give up and let the narcissist have his way, you are still making a decision, which often doesn't benefit you or others in your family.

Integrity and self-esteem are at the core of decisions that you're proud of and that are consistent with your values. From now on, be aware and mindful of the decisions you are making in your life. Every yes and no you put out into the world moves you down the path to where you will be years later. Pay attention to your goals and be cognizant of whether you are moving in the direction you desire.

Notice How You Feel Before Deciding

Sometimes decisions take days and months to accomplish, and other decisions are made instantaneously. As you go through this transition, notice how you feel during every step of every decision. If your response isn't a strong sense of *yes*, then you've probably not yet found the right decision for yourself. That doesn't mean you won't have any misgivings about whether you can achieve your goals—you can't predict the future. If the choice doesn't feel good to you, keep collecting information. Big decisions often include dozens of small decisions along the way. Pay attention to how you feel about each one, and you'll find your path.

Count Your Successes

Seeing yourself moving toward your goals and the life you want will help you feel stronger and more independent. Recognize and positively affirm each step you take—even the small ones. It can be tempting to just keep looking at what still needs to be done. When you acknowledge your satisfaction with what you've accomplished, you'll feel more enthusiastic and energized to keep moving forward. Keep your spirits and courage strong by counting all your successes.

You Can Always Decide Again

Few decisions are permanent. Don't get stuck because you think each decision, commitment, or new obligation is forever and can never be changed. New information comes to you every day that requires you to reassess whether your original decision is still the appropriate one. Change is the only constant there is in life. Adjusting decisions when new circumstances and new information become known will make you more adaptable and happier.

LOOK OUT FOR YOURSELF

Keep Your Own Best Interests in Mind

Caretaking results from an imbalance in giving and receiving. That does not mean that you should stop giving, helping, and accommodating the needs of others. However, it does mean you should be equally aware of your own needs and interests. When you're giving to others, notice what you're feeling in the moment and afterward. Those who are appreciative will give you a very different feeling than those who take you for granted or feel entitled. You have a right to decide how much you give, to whom, and how often. Put your energy where it will be valued and welcomed, and don't be blackmailed or coerced by social guilt, emotional threats, or pressure to give more than you want.

Allow Others to Be Strong

You don't always have to do everything yourself. Ask for help when you need it. That allows others to feel valued and helpful. However, be careful who you ask. The end of your relationship means that it's no longer appropriate to ask for extra favors and special consideration from the narcissist. That will just lead to hostility, anger, and disappointment. Let family and friends give to you when you need help. Don't think independence means you have to be stoic, totally self-sufficient, and reject considerate offers from others. Acceptance may be a good way to learn a better balance in relationships.

CONCLUSION

Becoming independent is a combination of listening to your feelings and needs, caring for yourself, visualizing your goals, and investing in yourself. You may need to learn some new skills to deal with the problems that appear, but every time you're successful, you'll feel stronger and more competent. Passively waiting for someone else to see what you need and take care of it for you is not a viable option for happiness. There are so many possibilities available in the world just waiting for you, but you have to have the courage to make new decisions and take new actions to move forward.

QUESTIONS FOR REFLECTION

What codependent behaviors did you have with the narcissist?

Do you know what your goals and passions are? How could you find out more about these?

What fears keep you from being independent? From voicing your needs? From sharing your feelings?

Try out the problem-solving techniques on a current problem. What did you discover?

How accurate is your intuition? Do you feel that you trust your intuition enough?

How well do you congratulate yourself and enjoy your successes? How could you do this more?

Overall, how independent do you think you are at this time?

When do you let others help you? What do you believe you should be doing on your own?

What advantages would there be for you if you became more independent?

V

Transform Your Life

NEW WAYS OF LIVING AND LOVING

When you quit taking on the caretaker role in a relationship, you will greatly reduce your likelihood of getting into another relationship with a narcissist. You will be able to see the signs of narcissism more easily, even when the narcissist is trying to hide them from you. And since you won't be jumping in to respond to the narcissist's tests, you will no longer be as attractive to narcissists. In addition, your self-esteem will be high enough that the narcissist's lure of taking over your life with his charm will not be appealing to you.

In this last section, we will be exploring the process of forgiveness. It is the last step in putting your past relationship to rest. Forgiveness isn't done for the other person; it is really a process that allows you to fully let go and move on with your life. Forgiving a narcissist is a unique experience because the narcissist will continue doing his selfish and hurtful behaviors. This is not a one-time behavior you are dealing with but a continuing pattern. Even though forgiveness may take years, it is worth the effort.

There is also a chapter on techniques for releasing the past, which brings together all that we have covered in previous chapters. After you have healed, your willingness to be in your life as it is now unleashes energy and enthusiasm. It opens up opportunities to create a life that is more to your liking and more reflective of your unique talents, abilities, and interests. You may even begin to contemplate the fact that the end of this relationship was one of the most important and growth-promoting experiences of your life. It opened the door to your being more of who you are. You are changed. You are stronger. You are more aware.

You are ready to reach out and find deeply loving friendships and love relationships that can really fulfill your dreams. When you love and appreciate yourself, you create loving energy for others. Being open to loving again can be scary considering what you have experienced. When you stay aware of the red flags and are already headed down the path you want your life to follow, you have a much greater probability of success. Knowing what real love looks like and feels like gives you the criteria to make positive choices.

Where your life is headed depends on your intentions. When you know what your goals are, you have a greater possibility of reaching them. Repurposing your dreams and rewriting the old messages you grew up with can bring you closer to your true life direction. It is in your hands.

15

FORGIVENESS

"Life's purpose of happiness can be gained only if people cultivate the basic human values of compassion, caring and forgiveness."
—The Dali Lama

Forgiveness is a natural stage in the process of healing. It begins when you give up your resentment and need for revenge or payback. Forgiveness usually comes when you're close to feeling whole and reconciled with what has happened and you're ready to let the past be as it was and move forward. It helps to have an understanding of what happened and why so you can place what you've gone through in perspective. And finally, when you've found meaning in your pain and suffering, forgiveness occurs more easily. Obviously, this takes time.

Pushing yourself to forgive before you are ready only makes you feel unworthy, guilty, and inadequate. Many years working with clients has made it clear to me that forgiveness doesn't happen until you reach *acceptance* of the narcissist and yourself just as you are. Too often people try to force themselves to forgive before they are healed. Let yourself go through the entire process of grief and healing. After you have seen the full scope of your relationship with the narcissist, you'll have a better idea of what you are forgiving the narcissist for and also be able to forgive yourself for being taken advantage of. They go together.

EMPATHY

Empathy Versus Sympathy

Empathy is a significant element in the process of forgiveness. However, empathy is easily confused with sympathy, and sympathy is *not* an effective way to reach forgiveness. Empathy is the deep understanding of and compassion for another person's feelings, reactions, and experiences, whereas sympathy is actually experiencing the other person's feelings and perspective. Caretakers are very good at sympathizing, but true empathy can be more elusive. In sympathy, you are joining and going into the emotional experience of the other person. When the narcissist was sad, you felt miserable too; when he was angry, it triggered your anger; when he felt lonely, you felt responsible. Sympathy pulls you into the experience, and as a result, you become part of the drama. It can eventually trigger resentment in you because the other person isn't appreciative enough of your efforts. Real empathy doesn't activate resentment or a need for repayment.

Empathy Requires Boundaries

Empathy is actually harder to do because it requires you to keep your boundaries. You remain one step out of the drama. You are tuned in to the other person with deep compassion while endeavoring to understand his or her feelings. Staying that one step away allows you to be compassionate without being drawn in to play a part in the drama. This is exactly what therapists train for years to do. It is also why being empathetic with people you deeply love and are emotionally enmeshed with is extremely difficult. Narcissists expect and demand sympathetic responses from their loved ones. They want you to feel what they are feeling. They want their pain to be your pain. To forgive the narcissist, you'll have to be able to step out of the drama and see the experience with some objective perspective and understanding. It is also hard to reach forgiveness when the narcissist's selfish behaviors are still causing you pain.

Janice thought that she was being empathetic to Jason's explanations about not being able to send all of her support payments on time. His checks were coming later and later in the month until one month she didn't get a check. After talking with her therapist, she realized that she actually felt sorry for him and not empathy. She had not been paying enough attention to her own needs. She notified the district attorney and had the payments made through the court. Later she found out he didn't send the last check because he had used the money for his honeymoon in Hawaii. Her sympathy had allowed her to be hurt again.

Empathy Is Nonjudgmental

Empathy also requires you to be nonjudgmental. There is no criticism in true compassion. As you work on forgiving the narcissist and yourself, you need to be aware of any hurts and offenses that you're still hanging onto and let them go. Letting go is not the same as forgetting. It means you no longer replay the hurtful experiences over in your mind to get that jolt of righteous anger or, conversely, to fuel your sympathetic reconnection with the narcissist. Condemning yourself or the narcissist does neither of you any good in the present. It will not erase what happened, nor will it keep you safe in the future.

Being nonjudgmental is an enormous challenge. You counted on the narcissist for love, caring, emotional and financial support, companionship, and acceptance, and the narcissist did not fulfill his promises and commitments to these things. This was hurtful and damaging to you and had a permanent effect on your life. It's hard to let go of your sense of maltreatment and negligence when you're still interacting or depending on the narcissist for anything.

When you see and accept the emotional disability that is at the heart of narcissism, it can make it easier to be less judgmental. You don't have to let go of your real observations, negative evaluations, or even your dislike of the narcissist's behaviors. Forgiveness is more of a neutral stance in which you no longer honestly care about the narcissist in relation to yourself. You can see him from a distance, rather like the stranger he is.

Acceptance and Empathy

So how do you accept the narcissist? By now, you may have read several books or searched the Internet for information on understanding the narcissist. This book is designed to help you understand *your* experiences with the narcissist. Your relationship with the narcissist is or was a complicated dance based on delusion and confusion. To accept the narcissist, it helps to understand that you and the narcissist are quite different in how you view the world, relationships, love, commitment, caring, and much more. And your two viewpoints will never come together. The narcissist isn't likely to understand you, nor is he likely to change.

Being empathetic means seeing and holding in your mind these differences while at the same time acknowledging your common humanity, fallibility, and the psychological disturbance that is or was a part of your relationship. You have the ability to change what you do and become more emotionally healthy, but the narcissist will probably always be handicapped and stunted in his ability to do so. Acknowledging the narcissist's damaged logic, low empathy, and faulty insight can help you move to a more compassionate stance without losing your own point of view.

Andrew kept trying to get "closure" with his narcissistic former wife, Rhonda. He wanted her to tell him what he had done to make her so hostile, blaming, and mean to him. He also wanted her to understand how he felt when she had acted that way. It was a struggle for him to comprehend that she had no idea why she acted the way she did. Each time they had a conversation, she would give him entirely different explanations for her behavior. Usually, the talks left Andrew more confused than before.

With the help of the Caretaker Recovery group, Andrew came to understand the mental illness of narcissism. He realized that Rhonda didn't know and couldn't explain why she acted the way she did. He had been feeling angry and hurt in their conversations, but after the group meetings, he mostly thought of her as disabled and emotionally immature.

TRYING TO UNDERSTAND

Motivation—Intentional Versus Accidental

Usually it's much easier to forgive accidental behaviors than intentional ones. However, it's very difficult, even for professionals, to sort out which of the narcissist's behaviors are due to their poorly functioning brain wiring, what they have learned they can get away with, or what they do on purpose just to get their own way. You have no ability to make the narcissist change, and he has little chance of significant self-understanding. So this confusion will probably remain.

Mental Illness

Narcissism is considered to be an "enduring and pervasive"[1] mental illness. Without insight, enormous determination, and constant self-surveillance of their behaviors, narcissists cannot make the changes that would be necessary for them to give you what you would rightfully expect in a reciprocal relationship.

When you've been directly and negatively affected by these narcissistic responses, it may be difficult to have compassion for the narcissist's frantic, frightened, and delusional world. It's easier to reach forgiveness when you can separate your life from the narcissist's. When you have more distance and can keep your emotional boundaries, you can see and feel compassion for the narcissist's emotional illness more easily.

It Feels So Personal

Keep reminding yourself that nothing the narcissist says, does, feels, or thinks has anything to do with who you are or what you've done. Your best emotional protection is never to take anything—negative or positive—that the narcissist says or does as the real truth about yourself. Instead, rely on your own observations and the responses and feedback from friends and family who are emotionally healthy. When you disengage your self-esteem from the effect of the narcissist, you'll find yourself on more solid and sane footing. Knowing that narcissists are a whirling dervish in their own made-up world can help you move toward forgiveness.

ACCEPT HUMAN FRAILTY

No One Is Perfect

Coming to a sense of forgiveness is easier when you remember that no one is perfect. The narcissist has treated you badly, but you also know that you have not been your best self around him either. As you get to a point of restored wholeness and healing, it'll be easier to forgive such huge shortcomings and defects in the narcissist, as well as your own defensive reactions.

If you aren't ready to forgive yet, don't scold or judge yourself or demand that you get there right now. Be accepting of where you are. Acceptance of yourself "as you are" is a great foundation for eventual forgiveness. Remember that acceptance does not mean you agree with or condone these behaviors. Rather it is a state of no longer protesting, demanding, or expecting the narcissist to be anything other than who he is.

What Part Did/Do You Play?

Because caretakers are usually too eager to accept responsibility for "making" the narcissist behave negatively, understanding your part in the drama is tricky. The narcissist behaves the way he does because of his own thoughts, feelings, and choices. So do you. Yes, it's easy to get pulled into demented and dysfunctional interactions with the narcissist, but you have a much greater ability to act differently than the narcissist does. You have greater control over your behavior, and you don't have the narcissist's delusions.

When you no longer feel susceptible to the narcissist's manipulation, insults, and biased opinions, you're on the path to forgiveness. You may be surprised that taking responsibility for your own reactions around the narcissist can give you insight, confidence, and the courage to protect yourself better and be more forgiving. As you feel stronger and more in control of your life, you'll find that you are more compassionate and able to forgive the frailties of others.

Juanita hated the fights she used to get into with Manny. He would call her names or demean her suggestions, and she would instantly be angry and shout at him. It wasn't until after they were divorced that she understood how insecure and intimidated she had felt around him. When Juanita heard stories about his volatile moods from her two adult daughters, her anger would flare up again. However, the girls didn't get upset with their dad the way Juanita did. They'd just stay away from him when he was aggravating and then enjoy being with him when he was more positive. Eventually, Juanita saw that she'd been using anger to protect herself from pain and vulnerability. When she became more disengaged and cared less about Manny's opinions of her, she no longer needed anger to protect herself. It dwindled away, and so too did her old pain.

Practicing Humility

Not only did the narcissist grow up with other narcissists, but you too most likely grew up in a family with a parent or grandparent who had a personality disorder or similar behaviors. You probably learned during childhood to accommodate, adapt, and resign yourself to crazy relationship patterns. However, a big difference is that you didn't inherit the brain wiring and emotional dysfunction that keeps the narcissist so mired in his contrary and skewed thinking and reacting. If you have a family member with a personality disorder, you were just plain lucky not to have inherited the same disability. You can see the misery he has in his life and the misery he causes for others. You've had many challenges caused by the narcissist in your life; however, I doubt that you'd ever choose to exchange places with him. You can get away from the effects of those inner demons, but the narcissist can't.

LET GO OF GRIEVANCES

Let Go of Trying to Control and Punish

Forgiveness includes letting go of trying to control or punish the narcissist for his behaviors. You definitely need to protect yourself from future harm as much as possible. However, trying to change narcissists, giving them ultimatums, or stipulating behaviors that must be accomplished before you forgive only keeps you entangled in continuing turmoil and dysfunction. It isn't your job, nor is it possible, for you to make the narcissist see his mistakes or change his behaviors. Forgiveness isn't dependent on the other person's shaping up or changing. You are not the monitor of the narcissist's behavior. Forgiveness is about your letting go.

Release Your Shame and Guilt

You'll continue to be caught up in shame and guilt if you continue to think you're responsible for the narcissist's moods and behaviors. When you fully realize that the narcissist's opinions and perspective are no longer important to you, your shame and guilt will soften and dissolve. Forgiveness comes from a place of acceptance of yourself and the other person. There is no room for disgrace, humiliation, or culpability. Keep checking on how your shame and guilt are healing and dissolving, and notice how you feel stronger as you let them go.

Let Go of Resentment and Revenge

Resentment and revenge feelings eat at your well-being and do nothing to change anything about the narcissist. Any strong, negative feelings you have toward the narcissist will be used by him to keep you attached and enmeshed. Once you become the narcissist's enemy, he will enjoy seeing you upset and angry. Narcissists feed off *any* energy, both negative and positive, that you send in their direction. You may think you'd get a feeling of satisfaction from seeing the narcissist crushed, but that's usually short-lived and doesn't make a difference in your future. Moving on with your own life toward love, joy, and contentment is your best revenge.

FIND NEW MEANING

Finding new meaning and purpose in your life as the result of what you've suffered can help a great deal toward moving you in the direction of forgiveness. Writing about this disorder and offering help to others who have been harmed by it have led me to a deeper understanding of my own experiences and increased my strength and resilience tremendously. Robert Enright, prominent researcher and author on forgiveness, says,

> there are many ways to find meaning in our suffering . . . focus more on the beauty of the world or decide to give service to others in need . . . speaking your truth . . . strengthening your inner resolve . . . [and] use your suffering to become more loving and to pass that love onto others. Finding meaning, in and of itself, is helpful for finding direction in forgiveness.[2]

What insights, new competencies, and greater understanding, strength, and compassion have you gained in this process of healing? If you have trouble seeing those for yourself, ask your friends and family to help you make a list. Validating what you've gained helps your healing more than looking at what you've lost. When you see yourself as tougher, firmer, and stronger, you'll find that forgiveness is more natural.

You're now learning more about yourself than you may have ever wanted to learn. What are you going to do with this new information? How can you use these new insights to make your life and the lives of others better? What opportunities have opened up? What new directions for your energies and abilities are you discovering? How can you use these challenging experiences to put what you have learned to good use?

GETTING TO FORGIVENESS

The forgiveness of others, and especially the narcissist, is important for your complete healing. You may find yourself able to forgive certain words or actions but not others. Take it one piece at a time. Forgive what you can, and keep working on letting go. Some things can take years to fully release. For example, one client couldn't forgive her former husband for teasing and demeaning her children until they reached adulthood. Only after she had evidence that they were strong, capable, and not indelibly harmed could she finally let go of her anger and reach forgiveness.

Forgiveness Changes You, Not the Other Person

Forgiveness may help the other person, but primarily it makes important changes in you. It is the final step in your healing. When you forgive another person, something inside of you lets go of the final piece of victimization. It probably won't completely eliminate your hurt or even all of your anger, although it might. It's an act that comes from strength and also gives you strength. It facilitates letting go of your ruminating, hostility, and rage. Continually thinking about a past injury will keep that memory in the present, whereas forgiveness lets it go. Forgiveness brings you to peace and allows the hurtful event to recede into your memory, where it should be.

You do not need to tell the narcissist that you forgive him. In fact, I don't recommend it. An angry narcissist will use it against you at some point, and a narcissist who has moved on doesn't care. Narcissists don't think they have done anything that warrants forgiveness anyway, so what's the point? Narcissists tend to be enraged or dismissive of your efforts, and that response can be newly damaging.

Forgiving Yourself

Forgiveness is a two-part process. You forgive others when they have harmed or victimized you, but being victimized in this highly independent and self-sufficient culture almost always brings feelings of guilt and shame. You may be angry at yourself for being gullible, taken in, or misused. Undoubtedly, you also had your own defensive, angry reactions to the narcissist's behaviors that you feel guilty about.

It may help you to know that even trained professional therapists are regularly manipulated by narcissists and respond inappropriately. Narcissists are clever and highly motivated to break down your emotional defenses. They are excellent actors and amazingly talented at protecting themselves. They fully believe that everyone else is responsible for how they feel and what they do, so no arguing or logic will sway their opinions. You end up feeling infuriated and foolish.

How many other people do you know who have been deceived and misled by the narcissist in your life? Do you think those people are stupid, foolish, or daft? Do you judge them for falling under the thrall of the narcissist's charisma? If you find yourself criticizing or judging them negatively, then you are probably still feeling victimized and will need to continue to work on forgiving yourself. Keep working on seeing your strengths and valuing your gains while letting go of your shame and guilt. This process can take more time than you might expect.

MOVING ON

It's Not About Forgetting

I do *not* think the old adage "Forgive and forget" is a wise choice for caretakers. Narcissists like to gloss over their misbehaviors, deny the hurt they have caused, and lure you into feeling guilt or shame for your reactions. You do not want to get lulled into thinking the narcissist will be nicer in the future. As long as the narcissist is in your life in any way, be prepared to deflect, disengage, and protect yourself from potential harm. One of the reasons you stayed so long in this manipulative relationship was your mental collusion to diminish and forget the narcissist's injurious behaviors. It will continue to be important that you are aware the narcissist will keep behaving just as he always has. Don't expect anything different until, and if, you ever see *long-term* changes in his moods and behaviors. Forgiveness doesn't mean that you forget the reality of the narcissist's dismissive and hurtful behaviors. Always be prepared.

Anger Doesn't Protect You

You may think you want to hold on to your anger to protect yourself from ever being tricked or controlled again. Anger does not protect you. You were probably frequently angry throughout your relationship with the narcissist, but that anger didn't keep you from getting hurt, nor did it stop the narcissist's behaviors.

Anger is a strong energetic emotion. It can get you motivated and activated to take care of yourself; leave the relationship; or to take on new and scary endeavors, such as getting a job, moving out, and being on your own. However, when you're angry *at* the narcissist, you're still attached, connected, and entangled with him. Continued anger indicates that you're still emotionally involved with the narcissist. Disengagement from the narcissist's power and influence over your emotions and your life is the only way to effectively protect yourself. Forgiveness won't fully happen until your anger has dissipated enough that you no longer get strongly reactivated by the narcissist's new, obnoxious behaviors.

After you've forgiven behaviors of the past, it is your responsibility to keep yourself away from further damaging interactions. Your new strength, resilience, awareness, and understanding of the narcissist and yourself will be better defenses and protection than anger.

Moving from Victim to Empowerment

The amazing thing about forgiveness is that it moves you from feeling like a victim to being empowered. It's a position of strength and potency. It feels much better than shame, guilt, resentment, or fear. Acknowledging what you've learned and gained from this challenging and arduous experience can liberate and energize you to move forward. Forgiveness helps you relegate your anger and hurt to the past. It's over. Even if or when you have contact with the narcissist again, you're forever changed and a more resilient person. Your participation in his drama is over.

Disconnect Your Energy from the Narcissist

Emotionally disconnecting and walking away is the only way to "win" and the only way to end the narcissist's manipulation over you. It is your best protection from further harm and helps you regain power over your own life. It's hard to reach forgiveness with someone who is still doing the same harmful behaviors toward you, but when you stop caring and emotionally disconnect, you will feel safer, stronger, and more willing to forgive and move on.

CONCLUSION

Forgiveness moves you into the present, and encourages old, hurtful memories to recede into the past. Empathy and understanding help you see the disorder of narcissism more objectively. As you heal, you can also have compassion for your anger and reactions, and you are more able to let go of your grievances, guilt, and resentment. You may even find new meaning for your life. Forgiveness is for your healing and can come only when you are ready and able to let go.

QUESTIONS FOR REFLECTION

How much sympathy are you doing instead of empathy?

What boundaries do you still need to put into place with the narcissist?

What judgments are you holding onto about the narcissist?

What does the narcissist say and do that still feels personally about you?

What self-judgments and criticisms do you still need to release?

What responses or reactions to the narcissist do you want to stop doing?

What lingering resentments do you have toward the narcissist?

What do you feel when you think about completely disengaging emotionally from the narcissist?

What do you still need to heal before you are ready to forgive?

What strengths, skills, and insights have you gained through this process?

What new meanings and purposes in your life are you discovering?

16

COMING HOME TO YOURSELF

"Never let yesterday use up too much of today."
—Will Rogers

BE HERE NOW

Being in the moment is healing. It is also the only thing that is truly possible. You can't actually go back to the past and change anything, and the future isn't here yet. Although you can plan for the future, you're not in *control* of what actually happens in the long run. So this present moment is actually what you have to work with.

The present moment is healing partly because of what your mind tends to do with those lingering past memories and future imaginings. When you spend a lot of time thinking about the past, you tend to feel either nostalgic for what you remember as pure and wonderful, or you feel guilty for what you did—or for what you didn't do perfectly. On the other hand, most thoughts about the future are either fantasies that are likely to lead to disappointment or thoughts that bring up fears and anxiety about what might happen that you want to avoid. Spending too much time thinking about either the past or the future keeps you anxious and guilty and also keeps you from noticing what is happening in the present. This means that you're not here in reality, you're not paying attention, and you're not enjoying or dealing with whatever is going on right now in your life.

Living with the narcissist was all about the past and the future because the present was often too painful and confusing to deal with. The narcissist kept blaming you for his past mistakes while promising a new and more wonderful future. You kept trying to analyze the past to figure out what to expect next. You tried to hold on to hope for a future that would be better than you were currently experiencing. The present was the last place you probably wanted to be.

What Being Present Feels Like

To have a happier life, you need to relearn how to live in the present. The following exercise is designed to help you become aware of what *now* feels like. You might want to record it and then play it back so you can enjoy the experience.

Task

Close your eyes. Take a deep breath. Let your shoulders drop. Notice any sounds you hear. Notice the air on your skin. Now pay attention to how your body feels. Do a quick check in with each area of your body, all the way from your head down to your neck, shoulders, arms, hands, back, chest, stomach, hips, thighs, calves, and feet. If anything feels tight or painful just touch that area and gently rub it for a moment or two. Keep breathing as you do this.

Now notice whether you are in a safe place. Is there any threat around you at this moment? Is anything bad happening *right now*? Notice whether your body is relaxed or on alert. If all is safe, let your body relax out of its alert mode. Observe how it feels to not be on alert. If you can't relax very much, just notice that.

What feelings you are experiencing? Are you sad, depressed, or demoralized? Notice how these feelings are about the past. Are you anxious, worried, or apprehensive? These feelings are about the future. Try to be here in only this one moment, no thoughts of the past and no thoughts about the future. How does that feel? Take a deep breath and open your eyes.

Notice how your body feels after doing this exercise. Are your thoughts different in any way? How long did it take you to do the exercise? This is how quickly you can feel better. Being in the present moves you away from most of what makes your life unhappy—negative experiences from the past and anxiety and fears of the future.

It is unlikely that you're going to do that exercise every minute of the day, but you could do it once in the morning and then right before you go to bed. You'll find that you feel much more relaxed and aware.

Practicing the Now

As you practice being in the present, you'll find that you're more aware of what is going on around you and that you're less easily confused or fooled by the narcissist's crazy rhetoric. You'll be better able to identify what *you* are feeling, which then leads you to being aware of what you want to do in each situation. It will help you make choices that feel good to you. You're likely to notice that you actually feel better being present than you may have expected. So here is an on-the-go method to check in with yourself designed by Debra Burdick.[1] This exercise uses the acronym SOLAR, making it easy to remember.

- *Stop* and notice what is going on around you. Especially notice how you're feeling and thinking at that moment.
- *Observe*, identify, and accept. Observe what is happening and what you're feeling. Identify the behaviors, thoughts, and feelings that are happening, without making any judgments, criticisms, or decisions at this moment. Accept that what you're observing and feeling right now is true.
- *Let* it go. Don't get into a drama with the situation, the thought, or the feeling right now. All you need to do is say to yourself "That's interesting." Almost nothing has to be decided, changed, or solved at this specific moment. Let it be until you have time to reflect on whether it's even important to consider further.
- *And return* your attention to whatever you were doing.

This whole awareness tool can take only seconds to do. The step that takes the most practice is learning to *observe*—and *accept*. In the past, you would likely *see* a situation, or *notice* a thought, or *feel* a strong emotion, but you probably didn't do all three together. It's important to identify and name all three so you collect all the information necessary to decide later whether there is anything you want to do about what is happening. Acceptance is key. One way to help yourself *accept* without judgment is to start out with the word *yes*. Here's an example based on the SOLAR technique.

> Your former spouse is coming to pick up the rest of his belongings from your house. In the past you have worried for hours about seeing him. Your stomach would churn, and your mind would race through dozens of old memories and hurts. Just seeing him would make you feel horrible about yourself. So here is something to try instead.

- *Stop.* When you start to worry, stop and notice the thoughts and feelings you're having. Mostly you notice they are all about the past. Bring yourself to today, this minute.
- *Observe.* Identify the thoughts and feelings that scare you, such as *I'm so scared he'll say something nasty to me.* Notice this thought is about the future. Bring yourself back to the present. Instead of ignoring your anxiety or being ashamed or mad at yourself, just notice and say *Yes, that is what I feel.* Accept that he is likely to act the way he always has, and remember who you know yourself to be. *I'm anxious, but I can get through this. I know I'm a good person, and I don't have to believe anything he says about me.*
- *Let it go.* Remind yourself that it no longer has to matter what he says or does. You have already collected his things together. It will be over and done in a few minutes, which you know you can handle. You breathe, calm yourself, and do your relaxing techniques.
- *And return* to what you were doing before.

Now you can decide if you want to do anything more to help resolve the feelings you're having. SOLAR helps you see more clearly what you're thinking and feeling so you can decide what you want to do. You're no longer ruminating and spiraling into worry and anxiety and feeling helpless. You have brought yourself into the present, where you can make a choice about what to do. Perhaps your anxiety is so high that you don't want to be present at all when he comes to get his belongings. Maybe you feel you could handle things more comfortably if a friend, your lawyer, your therapist, or a neighbor were there with you. Possibly you feel strong enough to handle it on your own. Knowing what you actually feel in the present helps you decide what plan will be best for you.

When you have a plan in place, you can let the worry go because your thoughts are no longer being pulled into a fantasy drama about some horrific, imaginary unknown that might happen.

Beware of Distractions

There are a million ways to distract yourself from being alive and present in your life. How do you distract yourself? When do you use distraction the most? Do you perhaps try to avoid feelings that you don't like, such as needs you are ashamed of or hopes and dreams that you don't feel you deserve to pursue?

One client said she spent hours playing computer solitaire. I had her do the SOLAR exercise while playing solitaire to see what she could discover. She observed that she felt lonely, numb, and disgusted with herself. Instead of distracting herself from these feelings, I suggested that she quietly sit and observe them. She was too anxious to do that at home alone, so she sat in my office with her eyes closed and identified each thought and feeling that surfaced. I coached her to stop any self-criticism.

She discovered that she was, indeed, lonely, but far from numb. She was angry, hurt, depressed, and despondent. The act of labeling her feelings made her aware that she was an outgoing person who was shutting herself in her home for fear of meeting her former narcissistic spouse in public and having an emotional reaction. Together, we devised a plan for her to socialize with friends at home or go out with a group so she felt free but surrounded and protected by allies and supporters.

Distractions are OK in the short term, but if they become a habit, you're just putting off the inevitable. Your feelings and needs don't go away. If you don't pay attention to them, they get more persistent, or they go underground and can eventually turn into depression, self-doubt, and anxiety. That was likely the state you were in when you were with the narcissist. Your feelings and needs were invisible and rarely got any attention. Don't do that to yourself now.

Stop Tuning Out

In your relationship with the narcissist, you devised many ways to tune
out, avoid, discount, or devalue your own interests, preferences, and
needs. You were so willing to give in to the narcissist that you may have
even forgotten what you liked and disliked. It's time to tune in to yourself again. You can't expect people to read your mind or be able to guess
what you are wanting and needing. Make your preferences known. Ask
others for help.

One client who had learned never to ask for anything from her
former narcissistic husband haltingly and with some nervousness asked
her friend to water her African violets while she was on vacation. She
was amazed and relieved when her friend said, "Yes, of course. What
are friends for?" You don't have to give up your own needs to have
friends who care about you. Be who you are. Expose your special interests, your likes and dislikes, and your honest feelings. That is a great
way to sift through all the people you meet to find the ones whom you
truly like and who resonate with you.

RELEASE THE PAST

Woulda, Coulda, Shoulda

There are literally thousands of past interactions that you could look
back on with the knowledge, experience, and information you have now
and say I could have, would have, or should have done something different. There are many fallacies in this thinking.

- Those interactions and experiences made you who you are today.
  You couldn't do then what you can do now because you're now
  different.
- You've gained information and knowledge about yourself and the
  other person since then that you couldn't use at the time because
  you didn't know it.
- You're probably mistaken about the amount of power and ability
  you had then to change things—especially with a narcissist.

- You can't go back and change the past. This whole line of retroactive, negative self-judgment is a big waste of energy and just makes you feel bad about yourself.

What you *can do* instead is figure out what you want to do now when these situations come up again. Use the phrase "I will _____ or I choose to _____." Identify what you'll say or do in that instance. Then file it away for future use. I've noticed repeatedly that when you figure out a good way to deal with a situation that was difficult in the past, that situation rarely comes up again. When you handle problem interactions effectively, they don't tend to reappear as often. Chewing over old experiences doesn't help protect or prepare you to handle them in the future, but having a plan makes a huge difference.

What Are You Still Hanging On To?

Too much time absorbed in injuries from the past brings up hurt, guilt, and doubts that are typically not useful for moving on in your life. Hanging on to these old grievances is much more harmful than helpful. As you're ending this relationship, now is a good time to neutralize these old injustices. The following exercise shows you a way to reduce the effect of past hurts.

Task

Make a list of the old situations that still hurt and make you angry. Choose one to work on. What would you like to have said or done that would have felt better to you? Write down your new response. Notice how this new response feels. You can even go one step further and play out the *new* response scenario in your mind in a strong and confident manner. Whenever that memory comes back, replay it with your new response. You may be surprised that over time the memory may eventually change to the new version. Use this technique with the other hurtful memories on your list and see them dissolve into the past, where they belong.

Repurpose Your Dreams

Sometimes it's hard to release the past because it contains old dreams, hopes, and goals. Many hurtful experiences with the narcissist are about those dreams and hopes being ruined. You wanted a loving relationship, a partnership, and a feeling of safety and love. You thought you were building a life together, saving money for your dream goals, buying a home, having children. Many of these dreams were tarnished or demolished by the narcissist's actions. It's time to repurpose your dreams so you can discharge this pain and regain your hopes for the future.

Almost everything you wanted to do with the narcissist can be done on your own or with somebody else. There may need to be adjustments in the where, when, and how, but your core dreams are part of who *you* are and are not dependent on the narcissist. *You* are the fundamental source of these dreams. You just previously thought the narcissist was going to be a part of them. Even though the narcissist is now off in another direction, you can still move forward.

Task

One definition of a dream is something notable for its beauty, excellence, or enjoyable quality. Make a list—with specific details—of your fondest hopes and dreams for your life. Here's an example from one of my clients.

Dream	*Details*
Have a loving family	Loving means understanding, empathy, calm, safe, secure, and genuine.
	Family means people I'm related to or feel very, very close to. Marriage (Oops! That's a different dream.)
	Family means children. I don't have children. Now I'll probably never have kids. I really want to be around children. Whose children? In what ways can I be around children? Possible interactions

> with children: My sister has two
> boys. I also teach piano lessons to
> kids.

Using this list helped my client realize she had several viable and enjoyable options for a greater feeling of family. She decided to spend more time with her sister's family and her nephews, especially on holidays and vacations, and she began attending the boys' sporting events. She also remembered that she had had a dream of creating a community of piano teachers, students, and parents, which she had let go of previously because her narcissistic husband dismissed it as "stupid and boring." She designed several social events and recitals that brought people together and eventually helped raise money for scholarships for children who wanted but couldn't afford music lessons. Out of her loneliness and dream of family and community, she found a way to connect, enjoy companionship, and use her interests and skills where they helped others and were greatly appreciated. This didn't look like her original dream from her twenties, which was based on a husband and children of her own, but it fulfilled all of the basic elements of what she truly needed today, in her late forties, for a sense of family, contentment, and fulfillment. Almost every dream can be repurposed if you give it enough thought.

Other Exercises for Releasing

Intrusive, painful memories or thoughts can come up unexpectedly from your subconscious mind. That part of your mind responds and works more commonly in images or feelings, so symbolic gestures can often help to redirect and reprogram it. Here are some ideas from former clients.

- Box up all of your pictures of the narcissist and tape it closed. Put the box in storage until you are ready to let it go completely, burn the box, or throw the box in the trash.
- Rip up or burn your wedding outfit.
- Sell the presents the narcissist gave you. Use the money to do something fun.

- Clean everything out of your house that reminds you of the narcissist. Give it away.
- Block, unfriend, and delete digital references to the narcissist on all your devices.
- When old, negative memories come to mind, imagine clicking to a different channel.
- Buy a new bed, new sheets, and/or new dishes.
- Rearrange the furniture.
- Go to your old, favorite places with new friends. Make new experiences there.
- Start a new exercise routine. It's amazing how this can change your thoughts and feelings.
- Learn a new skill. Give your mind something new to think about.
- Now add your ideas.

Let Go of the Narcissist's Image of You

You're nothing like the picture the narcissist has of you. When you got involved, he created a dream image of you that was idealized and put you on a pedestal. The image had some of the qualities and traits you have, but it wasn't you. After the narcissist kicked you off the pedestal, his description of you was almost entirely opposite from the original picture. You aren't that image either. When you continue to carry around in your mind the narcissist's depiction of you, it will be difficult to see yourself accurately or to be free of your worry about what the narcissist thinks of you.

It's time to completely let go of the narcissist's image of you. That image keeps you trapped, like being in a circus fun house of distorted mirrors, and it's time to leave. As soon as you turn your back on those painful images, you'll feel relieved and more confident and accepting of yourself. You no longer need to care what the narcissist says about you because you're now connecting with healthier people who can easily see who you are and what you do. Just be yourself. Every time you allow others to see who you really are, the more they will like you. It reinforces that you're not who and what the narcissist says you are.

Task

Here's a way to let these things go. Imagine each crazy thing the narcissist has said about you as if each one were a tiny grain of sand. Let all of those grains of sand flow into a bowl. You might anticipate that the bowl would be heavy, but surprisingly it's not. Pick up the bowl in both your hands. Take the bowl to a place that you never want to go to again— perhaps a desert, or the North Pole, or the deepest point in the ocean. Set the bowl down gently. Turn around and leave. As you visualize this, I suggest that you actually pick up a bowl in both of your hands and then set it down because it will make the experience more vivid in your memory.

As Dr. Seuss said, "Be who you are and say what you feel, because those who mind don't matter, and those who matter don't mind." Good words to live by.

REDUCING FUTURE FEARS

What Ifs

Ninety-nine percent of all the *what ifs* that we invent never come to pass. Future fears are one of those pastimes that waste energy, create havoc, and expand your anxiety for no good reason. Having a plan and even a backup plan for your top couple of probable expectations is rational. Having a plan for every contingency you can imagine leads to high anxiety and immobilization.

Limit how much time you spend ruminating about possible reactions from the narcissist—or anyone else. Anticipating the worst keeps you from living your life comfortably and with enjoyment, and it does nothing to actually prepare you for what might happen. Typically, you just find yourself reviewing the same aggravating and upsetting scenes in your mind. This is a form of self-harm that you can choose to stop, but it takes determination and practice. Although these are only *thoughts*, not things that are actually happening now, your subconscious mind often triggers your body to respond to them as if they were real. This is exhausting and can cause chronic stress symptoms—all instigated by your racing thoughts. Getting over the habits of worrying and being anxious is worth the effort.

Anxiety doesn't just occur randomly. It's triggered by your anticipation of something vague and unpredictable happening at any moment. If you've spent many years on the edge not knowing what crazy or distressing thing the narcissist might say or do next, your entire mental and physical systems may be overresponsive, always on guard and ready to freeze or run away. It may take a while to dial down your overreactive alarm system.

Remember the SOLAR exercise about tuning in to the present moment and practice it daily. When you find yourself going to the past or the future, gently bring yourself back to the present. Don't be harsh or critical in any way. Find things that engage your attention right now so it's less tempting to let your mind wander. One client imagines an internal bell that she rings in her mind whenever she notices herself worrying or feeling anxious about something that hasn't happened yet or may never happen. It's her self-reminder to stop and move on to other thoughts. Each time you change your thinking from fear to calmness, the less anxious you'll be and the happier you'll feel.

Dial Down Your Anxiety

Self-nurturing and self-compassion are good steps for relaxing and lowering your anxiety. To fully heal, you need to take self-nurturing seriously and build it into your daily routine—not just for now, but forever. Think of self-kindness and compassion as medicines that you need every day to heal and regain your strength. You'll also need to use them in the future to keep yourself from returning to caretaking behaviors. What nurtures you? My grandmother believed that fresh grown, homemade food was what kept her mentally and physically healthy until she died at 101 years old. Here are some other examples:

- A ten-minute walk outside
- Music
- Hugging yourself
- Weekly massages
- Reading a book
- Calling a friend who listens

- Making art
- Quiet time with yourself

Task

Make a list of what nurtures you, and pick one thing to do for at least five minutes *every day*. Make a date with yourself once a week to spend a full hour doing something nurturing for yourself. Think you don't have time? Poppycock! Take some time away from taking care of everyone else and give it to yourself. It will give you more energy, joy, and much more enthusiasm and love to give to others than you had before. You have to fill up your own reservoirs of need before you have enough to give to others. Every time you give energy out to others, you have to replenish. One reason you got stuck in an unhealthy relationship was because you quit taking care of your own needs.

Your ability to soothe, nurture, and calm yourself is invaluable in lowering anxiety, healing, and maintaining emotional strength. Alcohol, drugs, smoking, overeating, or nonstop TV watching can be quick ways to calm yourself, but they'll eventually bring more stress and problems than they relieve. Try the exercises in this book instead.

Personal Safe Haven

Having effective ways to nurture yourself and creating an internal safe haven within are two powerful ways to truly protect and keep yourself sustained throughout whatever may happen. You can train your mind to create an internal sense of safety and well-being instead of using anything outside yourself, such as chemicals, food, stimulation, or other people. Try this visualization.

Task

Think about a place that feels safe, nurturing, and comfortable to you. Imagine you are there right now. What feels good about this place? Notice your body relaxing. Take a deep breath and relax even more. Bring to mind something or someone that helps you feel cared about and loved. As you notice that good feeling, help it grow and expand until you experience it all over your body. Select a nurturing word or phrase to remind you of this feeling. Hold on to these images and feelings as you take your right hand and run it gently from the top of your head, down your left shoulder, and on down your arm and hand. Now repeat this stroking action using your left hand, and move down your right side. Take a deep breath and place both hands over your heart. Cross your arms and give yourself a hug.

This exercise takes only seconds. Practicing it trains your mind to go to your safe place instantly even in stressful situations. Bring up the image of your safe haven; gently touch your head, shoulders, or arms; or say the word you selected and your mind and body will calm. It's your home base that you carry with you wherever you go. The more you use it, the stronger and more composed you'll feel.

Create a "Code of Well-Being"

According to Dave Ramsey, "When you base your life on principles, most of your decisions are made before you encounter them."[2] Use your principles to create a core set of rules, or Code of Well-Being, to guide your life and head you in the direction you really want to go. Too often caretakers use the rules and preferences of the narcissist rather than their own principles.

Task

You've learned a lot of hard lessons from your relationship with the narcissist. To create a Code of Well-Being, write down the insights and guiding principles you've learned as a result. Use words that resonate and feel empowering to you. Keep it posted somewhere, and add to it whenever you learn something new. You might also want to write down why each one is important to you as a reminder. These will be invaluable guides for the future. Here are some principles that former clients have shared:

- Never give more energy out to others than I am currently receiving into my life.
- Give others a chance to give back.
- Don't try to fix anyone else's life.
- Don't try to do the emotional work for others (e.g., read books for them, call a therapist for them, make excuses or apologies for

them, give them more chances than you would give yourself, or say it doesn't matter).

- Don't deny or ignore *any* feeling that comes up.
- Don't blame anyone else for my feelings.
- Never "go along" to keep the peace.
- Better to deal with the problem now than later.

You could also create a collage of images to represent each principle to anchor it more strongly in your mind. Ask a trusted friend or loved one to remind you of your standards when she or he sees you getting off track, if you feel comfortable doing that. When you keep in mind what you have learned, no one else can mislead, scam, or threaten you into acting any way other than what is right for you. When you know you're living by your Code, you'll be less anxious because you are ready to handle whatever comes up.

Finding Your People

For thousands of years, humans lived in clans and villages, where nearly everyone was related in some way. In each little group, people tended to look alike, talk alike, and have the same values and beliefs. It felt safe. Choices were made as a family about marriage partners, work, and property.

In just a few hundred years, all that has changed. Now individuals are required to make every life decision on their own. This has advantages, but it also has disadvantages, such as anxiety, the possibility for huge mistakes, and a sense of loneliness due to lack of community. Since you aren't automatically in a clan or village of like-minded people, you have to find your people, that is, your own sense of belonging, your own friends, career, spouse, and community. And because people move around a lot more, you may have to continually work to find your people. How to do this well has become one of the dilemmas of the "modern age."

Obviously, you've found out that narcissists are not your people. But who are your people? To find where you feel you really belong, you have to know who you are, what you want, what you believe in, and how you want to live your life. When you know these things about yourself, you'll know what kind of people you're looking for. Most people enjoy others who are similar to themselves, but who are enough different to be interesting, and who bring new information and talents into the relationship. I'll say more about this in the next chapter.

MOVING FORWARD

Appreciate Yourself

Gratefulness toward others can be a catalyst to appreciating yourself. Other people love, support, and help sustain you, as you do the same for them. You are just as important to others as they are to you. Appreciating what you give to others is essential to learning your value as a person. Most caretakers think they need to give five or ten times more to others than they receive, to be a good person. This actually means you are devaluing what you offer at five or ten times less than what you receive. This inevitably creates an imbalance in your relationships and can lead to your being undervalued and exploited. You need to know your worth and that you have a right to expect others to appreciate what you are offering.

Appreciating your value doesn't mean you're suddenly going to become boastful or demand that others thank you for everything you do. It means that you'll choose carefully who you give to. If your gifts are unappreciated, you simply stop giving to that person and give to others who *will* be grateful. Notice how your gifts are treated by others, and use that as information to move toward or away from relationships appropriately.

Task

In your journal, list the traits, qualities, skills, and ways of showing love that you bring to relationships. Turn each one into a positive statement about yourself, starting with the words *I am*. For example, I am

- warm and thoughtful.
- considerate of other people's feelings.
- a good friend.
- excellent at handling finances.
- funny.

- loyal.

You deserve to be appreciated for everything that is on your list, and you also deserve to receive these same things from others.

Rely on Your Strengths

It can feel daunting to think about being on your own without your former relationship or to think about finding a new relationship. You're finding out so much about yourself. You have undoubtedly found that you are stronger than you thought you were. You've gone through a tremendous loss, and yet here you are trying your best to understand what happened and learn what to do that would work better. This shows tremendous courage, resilience, and an inquiring mind. You're not a person who sits around moaning forever. You're someone who wants to get going, do things differently, heal your pain, and move on to a better life. You're someone who perseveres and is determined despite difficulties and troubles.

You're strong. You're repairing, restoring, and rebuilding. As you learn new skills and heal old wounds, you'll come to a greater wholeness. You'll feel more confident, and eventually you'll find joy again. The new choices you make in the future will be more satisfying and successful because you have done the work of healing. Life is definitely going to get better.

QUESTIONS FOR REFLECTION

How much time do you spend thinking about the past?

How much time do you spend worrying about the future?

When you did the SOLAR exercise, what did you notice?

How do you distract yourself? How helpful or hurtful are those distractions?

How much do you let others know what you are thinking and feeling?

What fears do you have about being more open and truly yourself around others?

What regrets are you hanging on to? How could you let them go?

What past dreams would you like to repurpose?

What do you still need to release? How do you plan to do that?

What helps you reduce your anxiety?

How quickly can you get to your safe haven? What does it feel like there?

What principles or Code of Well-Being have you identified for your life?

How can you become more aware of your value to others?

How much do you appreciate your strengths?

17

FINDING OTHERS TO LOVE

"And then the day came when the risk to remain tight in a bud was more painful than the risk it took to blossom."
—Anais Nin

LOVE OTHERS AS YOU LOVE YOURSELF

Caretakers believe that if they give enough love, they will be loved in return. This doesn't work with narcissists, who have a low ability to love others. Louise Hay, author of *You Can Heal Your Life*,[1] suggests that you fill yourself up with love, and then as you overflow, send that extra out to others.

This is love that won't deplete you, won't leave you empty and needy, and won't abandon you. If someone doesn't appreciate your gift of love, you just pull back, knowing that it will not leave you wanting because you are always filling yourself up. In addition, this method reduces fears of being alone, unloved, or rejected. How do you do this? There are three ways to fill up with love—be open to love from others, feel love from universal energy, and love yourself through self-care and a positive, compassionate attitude toward yourself.

Love from Others

Being around loving, supportive people who are interested in your well-being is important to your feeling filled up. Too much isolation, too much time thinking about the past or the future, and overgiving can lead to feeling empty and lonely. You need to get attention and validation from others—to be seen, heard, and responded to. Other people pull you into the present when you interact, which makes you feel alive and joyful. You exchange energy with others and feel rejuvenated. Accepting and allowing others to love you can do a lot to fill you up.

Universal Love and Energy

I also believe that it's important to have a conduit to universal love. You may call this God, or Allah, or Yahweh, or a Higher Power, or all-enveloping love, or universal energy, or whatever you choose. When you know deep in your heart that you belong, that you deserve to be alive, and that you have not just been left on this earth to fend for yourself, then you have access to energy that can carry you through hard times. This energy, however, can be hard to connect with when everything seems to be going wrong. You can feel very alone and empty then. Here is one way to get back in contact with that energy.

Task

Focus on your breath. Your breath is the energy of life that surges through you in every moment. Where did it come from? You have this breath of life just as everyone else on earth has it. Do you deserve it any less than anyone else? Every time you breathe in you are accepting this gift of life. Every time you breathe out you are letting go of that which you no longer need—carbon dioxide, hurt, sadness, stress, the past. Take a moment now to breathe. Get in touch with your own source of life.

Focus on your feet. You are standing on the earth, which provides you and everyone else support, food, and all forms of useful plants, minerals, and animals that make your life here possible. The earth gives this support to everyone without picking and choosing. It also gives you the oxygen that sustains your breath. Stand on the earth, breathe in, and let yourself accept this gift.

Focus on the sun and the moon. These planetary bodies make life on earth possible. The sun supplies unlimited energy to all—with no favoritism. The moon keeps our oceans alive and offers everyone a sense of being loved and watched over. Accept this energy as your birthright. Let it flow into you.

Now take a moment to thank the universe for being in such balance that these gifts were given to you and that you can depend on them every day. Take time to appreciate the fact that you didn't have to earn these gifts. They're yours for free and forever.

Each time you tune in and appreciate these things, you'll notice that it fills you with energy and expands your hope. That transfer of energy is available to strengthen you—whenever you choose. Rely on it to recharge yourself. Use this universal energy when you offer help to others. Fill yourself up and then give it out to others instead of using your own physical and psychic energy.

DEVELOPING FRIENDSHIPS

When you leave a love relationship, it is tempting to want to find a replacement as soon as possible. However, as you can see, the process of healing takes time, reflection, new self-awareness, and rebuilding. Investing in the good friendships that you have and developing new ones are at the core of this step in your healing. Relationships with friends can help you practice more equal give-and-take. You can open up and share deeper parts of yourself. You can try out new skills, such as setting boundaries, speaking up for yourself, and being more assertive. With friends you can see yourself more objectively, practice skills, and try out new responses.

It's important to have a solid set of friends before going back into a love relationship. You will need their support, as well as their observations, insight, and honest responses to evaluate anyone new who comes into your life. You may not agree with everything they have to say, but you can use this information to make better decisions as you move forward.

OPENING TO LOVE AGAIN

Your former caretaker role may have left you so exhausted and burned out that you think you'll never want to be in a relationship again. You may not trust your own ability to see who will and won't be suitable for you. On the other hand, you may be desperate to get into a relationship again to soothe your pain and loneliness. As long as you are in either of these states, you're probably not healed enough to choose wisely.

However, there will come a time when you *are* ready. When you feel content with your life and it feels full and joyful, you'll find yourself willing and able to share your life with another person. As you heal your emotional pain, rebuild your self-esteem, and learn to accept caring from others, you'll find the life you are looking for—or it may find you.

Fear, desperation, depression, and anxiety can all get in the way of your being open to love again. As you heal the pain from the past, you'll be ready to choose who to bring closer and who to move away from. Your principles will be guiding you rather than neediness or fear. Knowing that you can take care of yourself, you'll no longer be desperate to find someone to make your life OK. You can begin to count on your feelings to lead you toward people, experiences, and choices that will resonate with who you are and what you truly want for your life.

RED FLAGS

As you explore new love relationships always stay aware of your responses. Never discount any feeling that comes up. Consider your feelings, intuition, and keen observations, and use these to understand yourself and the other person. As soon as you notice any sense of things not feeling quite right, step back, observe, and give full consideration to what you are noticing. Here is a summary of the red flags I give out to my clients to help them spot when things aren't quite right in a new relationship.

Move away from the other person and evaluate your situation before going forward whenever you

- feel engulfed, controlled, or manipulated.
- see an emotional double standard in the relationship.

- experience your feelings being denied, criticized, or dismissed.
- feel unheard or not listened to.
- notice the other person always needs to be right.
- feel your self-esteem diminishing.
- see a need in the other person to control the money for his or her benefit.
- feel there is something "not right," for example, secrets or unexplained behaviors.
- feel criticized, blamed, put down, or discounted (often done jokingly at first).
- feel confused by "explanations" that you're given about hurtful behaviors.
- observe out-of-control, overly intense emotional reactions.

Any time you find yourself uncomfortable with how another person is acting around you, immediately take notice. Observe the behavior, notice your feelings, and assess whether the interaction is respectful, loving, caring, and considerate of you. If it is not, step away from the interaction, and give yourself time to reflect. It may also be wise to talk with someone you trust about the situation to get perspective and feedback. Then decide what you want to do or say. Take every new relationship *slowly* to give yourself time to trust your new skills and instincts.

You may also find when you move toward a new love relationship that your old caretaking behaviors automatically kick in. Keep a close eye on *your* behaviors as well. Be aware of when you do any of the following things:

- Give up activities, people, or goals that are important to you to be in this relationship
- Feel hopeless and helpless for seemingly no reason
- Forget what is important to you
- Find yourself giving in to keep the peace
- Condone behaviors that are against your values
- Do more and more for the other person
- Feel unappreciated for all you do
- Tell yourself you don't have any preferences or passions that are worth fighting about
- No longer easily express your thoughts, feelings, and ideas

- Try harder to please when you are treated badly
- Ignore or forget to take good emotional, physical, or spiritual care of yourself

These behaviors don't indicate that you should end the relationship; they're reminders of things to notice and think about. Assess whether the other person is inviting you to caretake him or her. On the other hand, you may be caretaking even when the other person doesn't need or want you to. Be aware of automatically jumping into caretaking responses, and take steps to change those responses. You may feel awkward and uncomfortable as you approach a new relationship without caretaking. Always be aware as you navigate a new relationship. Keep at it, and you'll find it gets easier. Finally, don't waste your time on relationships that aren't leading you where you want to go.

WHAT ARE YOU LOOKING FOR?

What *are* you looking for? Have you ever sat down and written out the qualities you desire in a partner or set up standards for the types of interactions you yearn for? Have you created a picture in your mind of how the two of you would work together, spend time with each other and apart, resolve differences, get along with each other's family, spend and save money, divide up chores, and experience your sexuality?

Talk About It Sooner Rather than Later

Don't wait until you decide this is a serious relationship to share your ideas and feelings about these things. Telling yourself to wait and see what the other person's ideas are is a caretaking response. The wonderful advantage of being open and clear about who you are, what you feel, and what you prefer from the moment you meet someone is that you zero in more quickly on whether the relationship will be compatible for you. It means that you can sort out what won't work early on before you get too emotionally committed. Then you're less likely to spend months or years trying to convince each other to see things your way because you don't really work well together. When you use the wait-and-see model, you'll already be emotionally and sexually involved before you even find out if the relationship has the potential to work for you.

A Stronger Relationship Model

Having a well-defined model of what you want based on your principles will help you sort through your options when you meet someone new. This gives you a solid foundation for judging the core elements of the relationship while providing for flexibility and individuality.

Partnership relationships tend to be more stable and durable than the superior/inferior model you had with the narcissist. They require two people who can contribute ideas, tolerate different points of view, and negotiate disagreements and have equal consideration. Because you'll be more aware of your differences, you'll also need to have good communication skills and flexibility. However, these differences have the potential to result in higher-quality decisions and greater longevity of the relationship.

Needy or dependent relationships such as between a narcissist and caretaker resemble the letter *A*—both people leaning on each other. This model collapses if one person steps away by thinking differently or wanting to do anything separately. The partnership relationship resembles the letter *H*. It's pretty easy to see that the H shape is much stronger and allows each person to stand on his or her own, while still being connected. Two strong, independent people bonded together can move forward more easily and weather difficult times much more effectively than two dependent people.

Be Careful What You Ask For

Think back and consider what you were looking for in a love partner when you met the narcissist. What was it that appealed to you about him? Make a list of these things and compare them with what you are looking for now. What is similar and what is different? Certain combinations of characteristics can be very appealing but are also very likely to bring another narcissist into your life. The following characteristics tend to bring along with them a high likelihood of narcissism:

- Extremely good looks

- Highly protective
- Hard driving, results oriented
- Desire to make or have a lot of money
- Someone whose job is about controlling others' behaviors or lives, for example, pilots, surgeons, lawyers, politicians, positions of great power
- People who work hard to be convincing, for example, commissioned sales people, performers, extreme do-gooders
- Always has to look sharp and perfect
- Overly generous
- High expectations for self and others
- Secretly a rebel
- Obsessive-compulsive

These things aren't always correlated to narcissism, so look below the surface at the person's deeper, more emotional responses. However, be wary and cautious.

Don't Overlook Good Possibilities

When you were being a caretaker, your tendency was to look for a partner who really needed your help or someone who would take care of you. Your emotional radar was more strongly tuned to those who were struggling and needing assistance or those who seemed powerful, influential, and in control. You may have completely overlooked and ignored the possible partners in between.

Clients who have been married to narcissists often say they find this middle group boring, uninteresting, mundane, and unexciting. However, that group also tends to be reliable, steady, loyal, and devoted. They go to work, help others, take out the trash with a smile, adapt gracefully to new or difficult situations, share easily, cooperate, and like working as a team. They typically enjoy relationships with a balance of give-and-take. They share the load and take you as you are. Were any of these qualities on your ideal list? I hope so, because there are a whole lot of these people in the middle available and willing to really share a life with you.

Amy had been married to a cardiac surgeon for ten years. She had everything she wanted—a fabulous house, expensive vacations, lots of beautiful clothes, and entertaining social events. However, Steve was demanding, distant, critical, and extremely egotistical. Amy had always thought she wanted a husband who could provide well financially, until that's all she had. She couldn't take the emotional loneliness anymore and asked for a divorce.

For a long while Amy didn't date at all. Then she dated a number of men using her old criteria, but she feared she was making the same mistake. One evening after the biking club's group ride, she and Josh, one of her biking friends, went for a drink. Amy confided that she was probably never going to feel brave enough to get into another relationship because she kept picking the wrong guys. Shyly, Josh said, "Why don't we go out? We're already friends. What would it hurt?" Amy had never considered Josh before. He was the director of a nonprofit organization that provided after-school programs for kids. He didn't fit the picture of who she usually dated, but she found out that he did match the list of qualities she wanted. They were married two years later, and they now work together running programs for children all over the city.

WHAT LOVE REALLY FEELS LIKE

Acceptance

The real core of love is acceptance. Feeling accepted just as you are gives you a huge sense of peace, trust, comfort, and self-confidence. You know then that you don't need to fear rejection, censure, or condemnation. Disagreements are only about different perspectives and don't involve superiority/inferiority, good/bad, insult, provocation, or wounding. Acceptance means that mistakes are simply a difficulty to be overcome together. Even when you disagree, you still know you are safe and loved.

Task

Take a moment to imagine a complete sense of acceptance. Take a couple of deep breaths and relax into a full sense of well-being. Think about a person (it could also be a pet) in your life who has fully accepted you exactly as you are. If no living person comes to mind, imagine a loving fantasy being or someone who has passed away. Feel that person or being looking at you with complete love, even knowing your imperfections. Feel the love coming into you and filling you up. Send your love back just as completely and fully. Notice how your body feels. What thoughts come up? Let your thoughts and body accept the love that surrounds you. Breathe it in and hold it in your heart. This is what total acceptance feels like.

Peacefulness

The most common feeling people have after this exercise is a sense of peace and contentment. Calmness, peace, and harmony prevail where there is genuine love. Again, this does not rule out differences of opinion, but these are accepted and worked out with caring for the needs and dignity of *both* people. No two individuals see, feel, and think exactly alike. A peaceful relationship doesn't depend on your being alike; rather it's about appreciating, valuing, and even admiring those differences, as they add to the whole well-being of the relationship. I love the phrase "the Loyal Opposition" as it's used in England. It basically means that opposing perspectives can come together to create higher-quality solutions, while remaining loyal to the core tenets of the relationship. Being peaceful comes from the attitude of caring, a desire for harmony, and respect for each other.

Respectful

Respect includes esteem, reverence, high regard, appreciation, and acknowledgment. It doesn't require agreement, giving in, or giving up anything. It means taking the feelings and values of another person seriously. Did you feel respected by the narcissist in your former relationship? When and with whom *have* you felt respected? The opposite of respect is disregard. When you feel disregarded or disdained, you are not in a loving interaction. When others show respect for you, they aren't necessarily agreeing with you, but they are still honoring your value, treating you kindly, and taking your needs and feelings seriously.

Encouraging

Love is encouraging. It inspires you to be your best. You feel reassured. Your spirits are raised up, and you feel the energy and courage to move forward. You certainly don't feel hopeless and helpless, as you did with the narcissist. You feel emotionally supported, fortified, and energized. Remember a time when someone gave you encouragement. It may have been a parent, a teacher, or a friend. What did that person say and do that felt encouraging? Make a note of the feeling. That is what you are looking for in a long-term love relationship.

Freedom

Love is about freedom to be yourself. That doesn't mean freedom to do anything you like—but freedom to be who you are, with full confidence that the other person cares about you just the way you are. You're free to have your own thoughts, feelings, values, dreams, and goals, and you know you'll still be accepted, respected, and encouraged by your loved one. The fear of being disapproved of or abandoned melts away. You know you are loved for yourself, not just for what you do for the other person.

Equality

In a loving relationship, neither person dictates, controls, or demands that his or her ideas and rules will rule. It's a joint effort to create a life together that is comfortable and supportive for both of you. You may each contribute different things to the relationship, but both receive equal consideration. As a result, power struggles and resentment become negligible. Neither person tries to control or dominate the other.

Task

Write down your thoughts and feelings about being controlled or controlling another. Think about a time when you felt controlled by another person. What do you wish that person had said or done differently? Think about a time you wanted to be in control of someone else. What were you feeling? What did you really want? What could you have done to be more in control of what you wanted without controlling the other person?

Equal Value

Loving relationships give equal value to each person. That is, the individuality, values, needs, and yearnings of both people are kept uppermost in all interactions. Suggestions and differences of opinions are discussed and even debated. However, a solution is reached only when the resolution fully considers the needs of both. This may take more time initially, but the ultimate conclusion builds more love, understanding, and connection. Because the argument is solved amicably, this method eliminates the need to come back to it repeatedly to try to get a better deal. Each feels safe, at ease, protected, and sheltered with the other. Don't settle for less than real love.

QUESTIONS FOR REFLECTION

Who already loves you?

What is your method of getting love from universal energy?

How do you show yourself love? What more could you do to be loving to yourself?

Who are your friends? Why are they your friends? Do you need to do anything to develop more friendships?

How ready are you to look for a love relationship again?

Which of the red flags do you tend to ignore?

Which red flags about caretaker behaviors do you need to watch carefully in yourself?

What specific qualities are you looking for in a love relationship?

Which aspects of love have you felt you were shortchanged on in the last relationship? What actions are you ready to take to find those qualities in a new relationship?

18

LIVING YOUR INTENTION

"There is no passion to be found in playing small—in settling for a life that is less than the one you are capable of living."
—Nelson Mandela

SETTING YOUR INTENTION

As you've read through this book, I'm sure you've been thinking about your own situation and trying to relate each idea presented here to what you've been experiencing. I hope you've found the ideas helpful and applicable. You may have even realized that the recovery from your relationship with this narcissist is exactly what you have needed to become the person you want to be. The path to reclaiming yourself takes energy, courage, and determination. You've probably learned more about narcissism than you ever wanted to know, and hopefully you won't need to use that painful education very much in the future. However, what you've learned about yourself is invaluable because you'll take that knowledge with you. It's the basis of creating the life you want to have now. As you figure out what's important to you step by step, you'll have many new opportunities to use those discoveries.

You're no longer a collapsed, hopeless, fearful caretaker. You know that your thoughts, feelings, and needs are important enough for you to spend your time and energy figuring them out and lovingly responding to them. Now it is time to set your intention for how you want to move forward.

An intention is basically a determination to act in a certain way. It's a resolve—a way to focus your energies—based on your principles and goals. It is not a resolution in the common use of the word. Too often resolutions are made because of what you think you *should* do. This is about deciding to honor, support, and respect fully who you are by being aware and present in *your* life. It's not about doing anything correctly or perfectly or doing it to please, fix, or help anyone else. It's about deciding to be alive for yourself. It's about doing things in a way that is fully congruent with who *you* are.

Release Yourself from the Expectations of Others

As a caretaker you desperately wanted and waited for permission, acceptance, and understanding from the narcissist. Now you see that you would never have gotten those things from the narcissist, no matter what you did. In a convoluted way, this actually releases you from ever again having to worry about winning the narcissist's approval. It's an impossibility, so that discharges you from wasting your energy on it any longer.

However, being the nice person you are, you'll probably also have to work on letting go of trying to please, fix, and help some of the other people in your life. Remember, what you do for others has value and you need to choose carefully where you spend that energy. You can take care of yourself *and* give to others, when you keep the principle of reciprocity in mind. Doing things *for* others or to *please* others creates dependency and hostility. Be an example to others by maintaining your boundaries, while still being open and responsive.

Creating Your Intention

Look over your guiding principles and the truths you have learned about yourself through the earlier chapters of this book. See whether you can put into one sentence the overall sense of these lessons. Here are some examples:

- I've decided to have a calm, emotionally safe home with loving, gentle people around me.

- I'm a caring, generous person, and I expect to be around other people like myself.
- I live a life based on my choices, not the choices others make for or about me.
- Whatever I give to others, I also give to myself.

These are intentions. They state a core belief, a goal, and a resolve to make it happen. They help you

- set the standards of what you expect and are willing to tolerate;
- keep your boundaries; and
- maintain a vision of yourself, which then becomes the basis for your day-to-day decisions.

Take Action

Intentions lead to actions. Even more significantly, intentions make clear what your actions will be, with very little effort in the moment. If you want a "calm and emotionally safe home" you won't choose to be around anyone who yells, picks fights, insults, or demeans you or does behaviors that scare you. Because of your intention statement, you'll know instantly what you want to do in a new situation because it will either meet your standards or it won't. If it meets your standards, you move toward the interaction. If it doesn't, you stop, pause, and decide how much to move away. You don't have to spend any time figuring out whether the other person will like your decision, nor do you have to figure out what the other person wants or will say or do. You just have to decide what you want to do about the interaction. Do you see how this saves an enormous amount of time, energy, mental processing, and emotional angst? This is much simpler than what you used to do.

It may not be easy to give up your old caretaker patterns. Although you understand the idea of choosing your own actions, you may still be confused when you get caught in a difficult or intense situation with the narcissist. You'll know that you're still focused on the narcissist if you are asking yourself such questions as "How do I get him to stop yelling?" "How do I get out of this relationship?" "How do I get him to change how he acts toward me?" Underlying these questions is a continued hope that you can take action and have the narcissist be nicer or give you permission to act or that you can make him happy about what you're doing. This is old caretaker thinking, and you'll be confused about what to do. In reality all you need to do is decide what *you* want and then take appropriate action. It's no longer about making the narcissist think, feel, or approve of anything.

Your actions for your own well-being shouldn't rely on the narcissist's doing anything differently. Your actions can be as simple as hanging up the phone, walking away, saying no, not replying to e-mails or text messages, or not inviting such a hostile person to your home. By sticking to your intentions, you simply don't participate in anything that doesn't meet your values and intentions. Then you're able to embrace everything else with energy and enjoyment.

Trust the Process

Being a caretaker was about trying to be in control of the situation, so it may be hard for you to trust that things will work out, especially because they certainly didn't work out the way you wanted with the narcissist. Instead of controlling your own life's direction, you were trying to control the narcissist's, which is pretty similar to trying to control the orbit of Jupiter. When you turn your focus to making decisions about your own life, you'll find things work out more easily so then it's easier to trust the situation and yourself.

Throughout this book I've been outlining a process that has proven to be effective in helping caretakers change their lives for the better. As with most new things, it may feel awkward, and you may struggle with it at first. But as you put these suggestions into practice, you'll feel stronger and more confident and also begin to have nicer people around you. I strongly believe that you can create a better life for yourself than you've had. I deeply hope that you trust in yourself and have the courage to take these steps forward.

GRATITUDE

Count the Good in Your Life

The quickest way to move out of feeling victimized and hopeless is to count the good in your life. Gratitude has an amazing ability to remind you that the difficulties and pain in your life are really only a small part of what is happening. The vast majority of the people in your life and the experiences you've had with them are primarily positive. When you spend too much time looking out for danger and disaster, you can forget what is actually working well.

Task

One way to get a picture of this good in your life is to create a diagram. Take a large piece of paper and write your name in the middle of it. Then in a circle around your name, write the names of the closest and dearest people in your life. Beyond that create a circle of the names of friends, acquaintances, and others who are directly supporting and encouraging you. The next circle of names will be people, organizations, and community members who are helpful to you. Create another circle in which you identify your resources, such as your job, home, money, transportation, education, and helpful experiences. The next circle includes the people and institutions that protect your rights, such as police officers, lawyers, courts, laws, advocates, and mediators. Finally, surrounding all of these circles are your spiritual supports, including your Code of Well-Being and your overall beliefs about good in the world.

Keep this diagram—your Circle of Loving Support—in a visible place, where it can remind you of all the good in your life and the support you have. If there are gaps in any of your circles, reach out and fill them with new people, being thankful for these new additions. Give yourself some time to experience a feeling of gratefulness for each person and entity in the circle, and notice the resulting effect.

The Benefits of Gratitude

The feeling of victimization diminishes for each awareness you have of the love, kindness, and support around you. You may need and want more support, but appreciating what you already have helps you feel worthy to reach out for more. You have value and importance to others. You're the only *you* in the world. Be grateful for this uniqueness. Gratitude increases your self-esteem and self-confidence. It can help you relax because you know who you can call on for support and what resources are available.

Gratefulness reminds you that you are not alone. You belong to a community. The narcissist tried to keep you disconnected from others. Now you have the freedom to reconnect. Humans can't survive or prosper alone. We're a species that needs to function in groups. We need other people. Let yourself reach out and ask for help and continue to offer help to others. Just try to keep it more balanced. We are interconnected. Gratefulness is the glue that keeps those connections strong.

Task

Like most things, gratitude increases the more you use it. Take time each day to look at your Circle of Support diagram. Let yourself feel the caring and support from each person by saying his or her name, remembering a kindness, seeing that person's face. Then send your love and appreciation back to him or her. Gratitude is a circle of giving and receiving. Keep it flowing. This only takes a few minutes, but it can change your day.

You may find it enjoyable to keep a gratitude journal. In it you record good things that have happened to you each day. Keeping such a record provides tangible evidence of positive experiences that you can review. Too often we notice the painful things that happen each day, but we don't take enough time to be aware of and deeply feel the many lovely things that also occur.

NEVER GIVE UP BEING YOURSELF

Be Exactly Who You Are

This whole book has been about being present and letting the essence of *you* come out and guide your life. Yes, that's self-focused, although not selfish. This time spent paying attention to yourself and giving yourself time to heal hardly compares to the hours, days, and years you've spent totally paying attention to the narcissist. It's time to rebalance the scales. *You* were not taking *you* seriously. You were hoping that pretending to be who and what the narcissist wanted you could change him and make the relationship work better. Of course that failed. But that failure has allowed you to reconnect with yourself. You are the only one of you in the universe. Who can do the job of being you, except you? There is no evidence that you'll ever get a chance to be you again, so have the courage to trust that you have something that no one else brings to this life. Offer it, share it, appreciate it, and let others enjoy it.

Allow Others to Be Who They Are

Giving yourself permission to be who you are and live the life you want makes it logical that you would be willing to let others do the same. Letting the narcissist go hinges strongly on your letting go of trying to change him. By now you have living proof that it can't be done. You can quit worrying about anything the narcissist says or does because you now have ways to protect yourself from further damage. As you heal, you'll find that the narcissist is less and less interesting and troublesome because you just don't care.

Be an Inspiration and a Role Model

When you live your life honestly and with integrity, you increase your own happiness, and you also become a role model to others to do the same. This isn't a book about parenting, but the best gift you can offer your children is to show them how to be strong, loving, self-caring, and able to stand up for themselves. As they watch you have the courage to change your life and choose healthier relationships, they'll learn to do the same. Knowing this may help you release any guilt you feel about bringing them into such a difficult family situation. Your positive, respectful, determined, self-protective, and effective actions demonstrate to your children how to do the same. When you value yourself, they'll also learn to value themselves.

As you heal and your life becomes more positive, happier, and full of caring people, you prove to yourself that difficult people don't have to ruin your life. You can be an inspiration to others who are facing hurdles in their lives as well. You have much to offer them just by being you.

CREATE A NEW LIFE STORY

Rewrite Old Messages

Earlier we talked about repurposing your dreams. Now I want to encourage you to actually create some new dreams. It's time to let go of your old life story and invent a new one. When your life changes, your dreams need to change. Take an active part in deciding where you want your life to go from here. Rewrite those old, hopeless defeat messages with a new, hopeful tone. Take each negative self-thought and switch it around with a new message of self-truth. Here are some examples:

Old	New
I am such a fool for believing what the narcissist promised me.	I'm a trusting, good-hearted person who believes in the good in others.
I'll never recover from this relationship.	I'm strong, and I have made it this far. I have the courage to make a new life.
I always mess things up.	I'm not perfect. I learn from my experiences, and I see myself moving forward to a better life.
If the narcissist couldn't love me, I must be unloveable.	I'm loveable and capable. I love myself and others love me. I'll make a good life for myself.

Remember, the words you say to yourself about yourself have profound power. They are the foundation for your attitudes, life decisions, moods, and emotional energy. Be aware of your self-talk, and make sure it's directing you toward the life you are moving into, not the life you're leaving behind.

Task

A vision board is a collage that shows—in pictures—where you want to go and what you want to do. You can use pictures from magazines, calendars, photos, drawings, stamps, stickers, or whatever you want. Combine them in a pleasing way, depicting yourself as you want to be and the life you wish to lead. Let it be a vision of how you want to feel, what you want to do, and the words you want to use to encourage yourself. Keep it visible as a reminder of where you are going.

Remember Who You Used to Be

Try to remember the things you liked to do before you met the narcissist or even earlier when you were a child. What brought you joy then? What fascinated you? What excited you? Now might be a good time to try some of these things again. Years ago, you probably weren't so fearful and careful of everything you said and did. Take a chance now to explore different possibilities and see what happens. Tell your inner critic to sit on the sidelines for a while and just observe. It can be there if you are headed for real trouble, but otherwise let it take a snooze.

Try Something New

The best way to create a new life story is by going out and living your life in a new way. Be around new people. Try new activities to find out what brings you joy. Try some Meet-Up gatherings. Ask your friends what they enjoy doing and maybe go along with them. Learn a new skill, try a new activity, expand your limits.

The end of a relationship can mean that you have to move or get a new or different job. You get to choose again. That could mean a new neighborhood or a new town or even somewhere across the country. A new job can bring new skills, new people, and a new rhythm to your life.

These changes may sometimes be scary, but they could also be the best thing that ever happened to you. New choices bring new opportunities. Use the insight and skills you've learned here to continually assess what feels right to you and what inspires your curiosity and enthusiasm.

Take Your Time Within the Time You Have

Try to let yourself consider your new choices calmly and without immediate pressure. There can be time limits on some of these important choices, but often the stress of new choices comes from *you* putting pressure on yourself. And, of course, the narcissist always wants you to hurry up and decide. Don't create more stress by putting pressure on yourself. It adds too much sense of coercion and strain. Give yourself time to breathe, contemplate, consider, check in with your feelings, check the facts, imagine yourself in the new situation, make lists, check with your trusted friends and advisers, and then decide for yourself. Always ask yourself "What do I want?" The choice is yours and doesn't have to match what anyone else would choose.

FINALLY

My hope for you is that each day, you'll be a little more of who you want to be, whether that is being more honest, more open, more assertive, more fearless, more genuine, more of just *you*. Keep your vision in mind, and trust your intuition to steer you toward your goals.

QUESTIONS FOR REFLECTION

What expectations from others are you still trying to meet? Who are you still trying to please?

What are your primary intentions for your life? What actions have you already taken to live your life based on these intentions?

If you were totally and truly who you are, how would your life be different?

Who are you still trying to direct and control? Why? What are you afraid she or he will do?

What actions could you take to protect yourself without oppressing the other person?

Who looks up to you as an inspiration and role model? How does that feel?

What new things are you ready to try?

How can you make future decisions with less fear and stress?

NOTES

1. IT'S ALL ABOUT *THEM*—NARCISSISTS

1. Johnson, Stephen. *Character Styles.* New York, NY: W. W. Norton & Co., 1994.

2. Johnson, Stephen. *Humanizing the Narcissistic Style.* New York, NY: W. W. Norton & Co., 1987.

3. American Psychiatric Association. *Diagnostic and Statistical Manual of Mental Disorders.* Washington, DC, 2013.

4. Baron-Cohen, Simon. *Zero Degrees of Empathy.* New York, NY: Penguin Group, 2011.

5. Ibid.

2. WHAT ABOUT *YOU?*

1. Fjelstad, Margalis. *Stop Caretaking the Borderline or Narcissist.* Lanham, MD: Rowman & Littlefield, 2013.

2. Rosenberg, Ross. *The Human Magnet Syndrome: Why We Love People Who Hurt Us.* Eau Claire, WI: Premier Publishing & Media, 2013.

3. WHY RELATIONSHIPS WITH NARCISSISTS ARE ALWAYS DOOMED

1. Baron-Cohen, Simon. *Zero Degrees of Empathy*. New York, NY: Penguin Group, 2011.

2. Ibid.

3. Porges, Stephen. *The Polyvagal Theory: Neurophysiological Foundations of Emotions, Attachment, Communication, and Self-Regulation*. New York, NY: W. W. Norton & Co., 2011.

4. Karpman, Stephen. "The New Drama Triangles." Paper presented at USA Transactional Analysis Association/International Transactional Analysis Association Conference, August 11, 2007.

5. Fjelstad, Margalis. *Stop Caretaking the Borderline or Narcissist*. Lanham, MD: Rowman & Littlefield, 2013.

6. COPING WITH THE END

1. Kohut, Heinz. "Thoughts on Narcissism and Narcissistic Rage," in *The Search for the Self*. Madison, CT: International Universities Press, 1972.

2. Ronningstam, Elsa. *Identifying and Understanding the Narcissistic Personality*. Oxford: Oxford University Press, 2005, pp. 86–87.

3. McBride, Karyl. *Will I Ever Be Free of You? How to Navigate a High-Conflict Divorce from a Narcissist and Heal Your Family*. New York, NY: Atria Books, 2015.

4. Ibid.

7. LETTING GO

1. Rosenberg, Ross. *The Human Magnet Syndrome: Why We Love People Who Hurt Us*. Eau Claire, WI: Premier Publishing & Media, 2013.

8. GRIEVING

1. Kubler-Ross, Elizabeth, and David Kessler. *On Grief and Grieving: Finding the Meaning of Grief Through the Five Stages of Loss*. New York, NY: Scribner, Reprint Edition, 2014.

2. Moore, Thomas. *The Dark Night of the Soul: A Guide to Finding Your Way Through Life's Ordeals.* New York, NY: Penguin Group, 2004.

II. LOVING YOUR *SELF*

1. Schaps, Eric. "The Role of Supportive School Environments in Promoting Academic Success," Center for the Collaborative Classroom at https://www .collaborativeclassroom.org/research-articles-and-papers-the-role-of -supportive-school-environments-in-promoting-academic-success.

I2. BUILDING RESILIENCE

1. Porges, Stephen W. *The Polyvagal Theory: Neuropsychological Foundations of Emotions, Attachment, Communication, and Self-Regulation.* New York, NY: W. W. Norton & Co., 2011.
2. Hay, Louise. *You Can Heal Your Life.* Santa Monica, CA: Hay House, 1984.
3. McBride, Karyl. *Will I Ever Be Free of You? How to Navigate a High-Conflict Divorce from a Narcissist and Heal Your Family.* New York, NY: Atria Books, 2015.
4. Weintraub, Pamela. "The Voice of Reason," *Psychology Today Magazine*, May 4, 2015.

I3. SELF-PROTECTION

1. McBride, Jean. *Talking to Children About Divorce.* Berkeley, CA: Althea Press, 2016.

I4. BECOMING INDEPENDENT

1. Deresiewicz, William. "The End of Solitude," essay published in *The Chronicle of Higher Education*, January 30, 2009. Retrieved from http://www. hermitary.com/solitude/deresiewicz.html.
2. Fey, Tina. *Bossypants.* New York, NY: Reagan Arthur/Little Brown, Reprint Edition, 2014.

15. FORGIVENESS

1. Task Force on DSM-IV. *Diagnostic and Statistical Manual of Mental Disorders, 4th Edition.* American Psychiatric Association, Washington, DC, 2005, p. 633.

2. Enright, Robert. "Eight Steps Towards Forgiveness." Adapted from *8 Keys to Forgiveness.* New York, NY: W. W. Norton & Co., 2015. Accessed through DailyGood.org.

16. COMING HOME TO YOURSELF

1. Burdick, Debra. *Mindfulness Skills Workbook for Clinicians and Clients.* Eau Claire, WI: PESI, 2013, pp. 59–60.

2. Ramsey, Dave. *The Total Money Makeover.* Nashville, TN: Nelson Books, 2013.

17. FINDING OTHERS TO LOVE

1. Hay, Louise. *You Can Heal Your Life.* Santa Monica, CA: Hay House, 1984.

BIBLIOGRAPHY

Altman, Donald. *101 Mindful Ways to Build Resilience: Create Calm, Clarity, Optimism & Happiness Each Day*. Eau Claire, WI: PESI, 2016.
————. *The Mindfulness Toolbox*. Eau Claire, WI: PESI, 2014.
American Psychiatric Association. *Diagnostic and Statistical Manual of Mental Disorders*. Washington, DC, 2013.
Bader, Ellyn & Peter Pearson. *In Quest of the Mythical Mate*. New York, NY: Routledge, 2012.
Baron-Cohen, Simon. *Zero Degrees of Empathy*. New York, NY: Penguin Group, 2011.
Beattie, Melody. *Codependent No More: How to Stop Controlling Others and Start Caring for Yourself*. New York, NY: Harper & Row Publishers, 2nd Revised Edition, 1992.
Berry, Carmen Renee. *When Helping You Is Hurting Me*. New York, NY: Crossroad Publishing Co., Revised and Updated, 2003.
Borcherdt, Bill. *Head Over Heart in Love: 25 Guides to Rational Passion*. Sarasota, FL: Professional Resource Exchange, 1996.
————. *You Can Control Your Feelings! 24 Guides to Emotional Well-Being*. Sarasota, FL: Professional Resource Press, 1993.
Braiker, Harriet B. *Who's Pulling Your Strings? How to Break the Cycle of Manipulation and Regain Control of Your Life*. New York, NY: McGraw-Hill, 2004.
Brown, Nina. *Loving the Self-Absorbed*. Oakland, CA: New Harbinger Publications, 2003.
Burdick, Debra. *Mindfulness Skills Workbook for Clinicians & Clients*. Eau Claire, WI: PESI, 2013.
Carter, Steven & Julia Sokol. *Men Who Can't Love*. New York, NY: Berkley Publishing Group, M. Evans & Co., 2004.
Deresiewicz, William. "The End of Solitude." *The Chronicle of Higher Education*, January 30, 2009.
Enright, Robert. "Eight Steps Towards Forgiveness." Adapted from *8 Keys to Forgiveness*. New York, NY: W. W. Norton & Co., 2015. Accessed through DailyGood.org.
Evans, Patricia. *Controlling People: How to Recognize, Understand, and Deal with People Who Try to Control You*. New York, NY: Adams Media, 2002.
————. *The Verbally Abusive Relationship: How to Recognize It and How to Respond*. New York, NY: Adams Media, Expanded 2nd Edition, 1992.
Fey, Tina. *Bossypants*. New York, NY: Reagan Arthur/Little Brown, Reprint Edition, 2014.
Fjelstad, Margalis. *Stop Caretaking the Borderline or Narcissist: How to End the Drama and Get on with Life*. Lanham, MD: Rowman & Littlefield Publishers, 2013.
————. *The Borderline, the Narcissist and YOU: Learning to Let go of Caretaking*. Online class and workbook. Caretaker.digitalchalk.com.

Freeman, Arthur & Rose DeWolf. *The Ten Dumbest Mistakes Smart People Make and How to Avoid Them.* New York, NY: HarperCollins Publishers, 1992.

Golomb, Elan. *Trapped in the Mirror: Adult Children of Narcissists and Their Struggle for Self.* New York, NY: William Morrow, 1992.

Halpern, Howard. *How to Break Your Addiction to a Person.* New York, NY: McGraw-Hill, 2003.

Hay, Louise. *You Can Heal Your Life.* Santa Monica, CA: Hay House, 1984.

Johnson, Stephen. *Character Styles.* New York, NY: W. W. Norton & Co., 1994.

———. *Humanizing the Narcissistic Style.* New York, NY: W. W. Norton & Co., 1987.

Karpman, Stephen. "The New Drama Triangles." Paper presented at USA Transactional Analysis Association/International Transactional Analysis Association Conference, August 11, 2007.

Kirshenbaum, Mira. *Too Good to Leave. Too Bad to Stay.* New York, NY: Plume, Reprint Edition, 1997.

Kohut, Heinz. "Thoughts on Narcissism and Narcissistic Rage," in *The Search for the Self.* Madison, CT: International Universities Press, 1972.

Kubler-Ross, Elizabeth & David Kessler. *On Grief and Grieving: Finding the Meaning of Grief Through the Five Stages of Loss.* New York, NY: Scribner, Reprint Edition, 2014.

Lander, Lorne. *The Lost Art of Compassion: Discovering the Practice of Happiness in the Meeting of Buddhism and Psychology.* New York, NY: HarperCollins Publishers, 2004.

Masterson, James F. *The Narcissistic and Borderline Disorders: An Integrated Developmental Approach.* New York, NY: Brunner/Mazel, Inc., 1981.

McBride, Jean. *Talking to Children About Divorce.* Berkeley, CA: Althea Press, 2016.

McBride, Karyl. *Will I Ever Be Free of You? How to Navigate a High-Conflict Divorce from a Narcissist and Heal Your Family.* New York, NY: Atria Books, 2015.

———. *Will I Ever Be Good Enough? Healing the Daughters of Narcissistic Mothers.* New York, NY: Free Press, 2008.

Moore, Thomas. *The Dark Night of the Soul: A Guide to Finding Your Way Through Life's Ordeals.* New York, NY: Penguin Group, 2004.

Morrison, Andrew P. *Shame: The Underside of Narcissism.* Hillsdale, NJ: The Analytic Press, 1989.

Porges, Stephen W. *The Polyvagal Theory: Neuropsychological Foundations of Emotions, Attachment, Communication, and Self-Regulation.* New York, NY: W. W. Norton & Co., 2011.

Ramsey, Dave. *The Total Money Makeover.* Nashville, TN: Nelson Books, 2013.

Ronningstam, Elsa. *Identifying and Understanding the Narcissistic Personality.* New York, NY: Oxford University Press, 2005.

Rosenberg, Ross. *The Human Magnet Syndrome: Why We Love People Who Hurt Us.* Eau Claire, WI: Premier Publishing & Media, 2013.

Schaps, Eric. "The Role of Supportive School Environments in Promoting Academic Success," Center for the Collaborative Classroom at https://www.collaborativeclassroom.org/research-articles-and-papers-the-role-of-supportive-school-environments-in-promoting-academic-success.

Shields, Autumn. *Living Your Life Alive: Learning to Listen and Follow Your Inner Nudge.* New York, NY: Aviva Publishing, 2015.

Smith, Manuel. *When I Say No, I Feel Guilty.* New York, NY: Bantam Books, Reissue Edition, 1975.

Weintraub, Pamela. "The Voice of Reason," *Psychology Today Magazine,* May 4, 2015.

INDEX

ABOUT THE AUTHOR

Margalis Fjelstad, PhD, LMFT, has been a therapist for over thirty-five years, specializing in the care of people who have been negatively affected by a narcissistic parent, spouse, or child. She grew up with a borderline mother and caretaker father and salvaged her self-esteem after getting divorced from a narcissist.

Her Caretaker Recovery groups have helped people understand the relationship patterns that occur with narcissists and learn how to get out of these manipulative interactions. Her goal is to help caretakers recover their self-esteem and self-confidence and move on to healthier and happier lives.

You can find more information and subscribe to her Caretaker Recovery Newsletter at margalistherapy.com. Dr. Fjelstad can be reached at margalistherapy@gmail.com. You can take her online class based on the content from her recovery groups at caretaker.digitalchalk.com.